JACKIE STEWART

WORLD CHAMPION

JACKIE STEWART

WORLD CHAMPION

TEN YEARS TO A TITLE

SIR JACKIE STEWART OBE & ERIC DYMOCK

JACKIE STEWART, WORLD CHAMPION
First published in Great Britain as "World Champion" by
Pelham Books Ltd 1970 ISBN 7207 0413 8

THIS EDITION
Paperback

ISBN 978-1-9993647-4-8

Book and cover design: Hocus Design

A royalty on every copy sold will be paid to Race Against Dementia, a registered charity in England and Wales number 1165559, and Scotland SC052594.

Website: https://ericdymockmotorbooks.co.uk/

https://www.amazon.co.uk/stores/author/B001HO9BQ2/about
https://www.raceagainstdementia.com

This book is dedicated to the
memory of Jim Clark OBE

Sir Jackie Stewart's Acknowledgements

My original acknowledgement to this book began "To the lovely Helen for her tremendous support and dedication…" There's no need to make any change. Her devotion went well beyond my first world championship. It continues through to this reissue of Champion Year with proceeds going to Race Against Dementia. Helen's loyalty remained unbroken throughout my 99 Grands Prix and a lifetime of making motor racing safer.

This original of this book was compiled in the late stages of the 1969 Formula 1 season. My co-author Eric Dymock and I enjoyed the hospitality of Trudy and Bob Quigley at their home at Burlington, Ontario, Canada. Our thanks went to International Financial Management (UK), which organised the publication for me and Eric, who had covered my career from Charterhall all the way to grands prix.

As ever I acknowledged the role Ken and Norah Tyrrell had played and continued to play throughout my career as a racing driver.

Champion Year, then as now, is dedicated to the memory of Jim Clark OBE.

Eric Dymock's Acknowledgements

The original edition paid tribute to Pelham Books, its executive Bill Luscombe. We now also acknowledge Emma D'Cruz, Contracts and Business Affairs Director Solicitor at Penguin Random House, Pelham's heirs who tells us: "We do not claim to have any ongoing rights to this book" and wishes us well for the support it will provide to Race Against Dementia. Grateful acknowledgement is also made to Zoë Schafer, at Motorsport Images, for permission to use photographs by Michael Cooper, Nigel Snowdon, David Phipps, Ian Norris, and Diana Burnett all colleagues and contemporaries. The original text has been very lightly edited and a few of my photographs added. David Phipps took me to the former railway bridge at Monaco for the practice picture on the jacket.

NB: Passages written by Eric Dymock are printed throughout in blue.

PART ONE: THE BUILD-UP

PART TWO: THE 1969 SEASON

PART ONE
The build-up

1.

Introduction:

Brief biography 1963-64

The better you knew Jackie Stewart when he was younger, the more you expected him to become a world champion. It seemed a logical, almost inevitable course of events. Only those who did not appreciate his strong personality and immense energy felt, and indeed said many times, that Jackie Stewart was going too fast too soon.

People might have had less doubt had they known he had already been a champion. Less heroic perhaps, but a champion, nevertheless. It was part of his training, part of his preparation for winning in 1969.

Jackie's self-assurance can be mistaken for over-confidence, but it is not. They are different. You cannot even say that self-assurance is nothing more than vindicated overconfidence. Success and Jackie Stewart's straightforward and well-merited confidence go together. They always have.

There are times when one or the other takes severe punishment. Stewart's success may look easy, his self-confidence can appear impenetrable. Yet he is realistic enough to remember defeats and disappointments.

His shooting career made him something of a local celebrity. His brother Jimmy had been a racing driver of great talent and much promise in the fifties. The family were well-known in the Scottish motor trade, they were reasonably well-off, with their own business, and Jackie enjoyed many things in life better than his contemporaries. He had travelled extensively at an age, and in a social environment where venturing outside Scotland was an important undertaking; travelling to Europe was a major safari. A journey to the United States was something unlikely to happen more than once, or perhaps twice in a lifetime. Jackie's cars were Austin-Healeys when his friends aspired to Morris Minors.

But then, only a few of his friends aspired to being champion anythings. The Stewarts were sought after locally because they were interesting people. They had all travelled. They shot and fished enthusiastically, and all of them, father, mother, Jimmy, and Jackie were congenial company. The father's influence on the boys was one of encouragement and pleasure in achievement, their mother's part was willpower.

As the local Jaguar dealers, they found good social contacts useful in industrial Dumbarton. The town is the home of notable Scotch Whisky, with industry connected to shipbuilding, and the activities which are replacing it all the way down the Clyde estuary where it stands behind the blunt, rearing mass of Dumbarton Rock.

Amongst the young car enthusiasts, Jimmy occupied a commanding position. He had raced at a time when racing drivers, even in international sports car races, paid for their pleasure. He had raced privately a Healey Silverstone and drove one of the first C-Type Jaguars for Ecurie Ecosse, the leading Scottish team. He drove in 1953 one of the pioneer disc-braked C-Types, and then a D. He drove single seaters too, a Cooper-Bristol with which he won at Goodwood and was lying sixth in the 1954 British Grand Prix, behind the

John Surtees, Roy Salvadori, Tony Brooks, Graham Hill, Stirling Moss. Big names were still on the pit boards the day 23-year-old Jackie Stewart made up his mind to join them. Aston Martin owner Barry Filer sets him off in early 1962. The September 1961 Oulton Park Gold Cup was won by Moss, a first for the four-wheel drive Ferguson on a damp track.

Ferraris and Maseratis of Ascari, Fangio, Farina, Gonzalez, and Hawthorn until he spun off in drenching rain. Philosophical but self-effacing, "I was mortified. It would have been great to bring the first British car home, but I blew it."

He went off only ten short of the full 90 laps. Had it possessed a podium, Jimmy Stewart came close to sharing it with four past, current and future world champions. He was only 22, had been halfway up the starting grid with a car still using downdraught Solex carburettors and invited to become a member of the works Jaguar team drove in the 1955 Daily Express Production Car Race at Silverstone. He was second to Mike Hawthorn in a Mark VII, but withdrew from racing shortly afterwards. He had been asked to drive a D-Type at Le Mans with Hawthorn that year, in which Hawthorn won. But he had decided to give up.

Jimmy Stewart was keen, competitive, polished, and very fast indeed. The boy soprano-turned racing driver had a promising career ahead. Stirling Moss, Peter Collins, and Mike Hawthorn had shown that Latin temperament was not essential for success (it was much later before it seemed a downright disadvantage) and Ecurie Ecosse had shown that drivers from Scotland could be a match for any.

Pressure from an anxious mother cut short Jimmy's racing. He had an accident in a works Aston Martin at Le Mans and severely damaged an arm. Doctors warned that further damage would be serious, so strongly influenced by his mother, Jimmy retired. He returned to the family business where Jackie, nine years his junior, having left school at fifteen, was employed as an apprentice mechanic.

The garage had a reputation for good if expensive service. A professional approach was a family tradition. The Stewarts would turn out cars from the repair shop, or the tiny showroom as well prepared as they could, but above all they always looked as though they had been in the hands of experts. When your car returned from a service at Dumbuck Garage, everything felt better. The family gave it a very personal sort of attention.

Stewart senior was kindly, generous natured, yet astute and determined. His sons seemed to inherit all these qualities. The proportions varied. Jimmy got most of the first two, Jackie predominantly the second two. Which is the main reason Jimmy gave up racing and Jackie did not.

Jimmy Stewart set lap times in the Aston. Jackie matched them.

As a teenager Jackie went to lots of races where his brother was taking part. He became a motor racing enthusiast. But as the time came when he might have wanted to drive himself, he set out to do something quite different. He took up shooting, an absorbing, time-consuming and quite expensive sport. Like Jimmy's racing it was mostly subsidised by his father.

By 1960, Jackie had won almost everything in the clay pigeon world worth winning except the accolade of a place in the Olympic team. The important thing for his future motor racing career was that it had given him the opportunity to be a success. He knew what it felt like to be a champion.

Every athlete or sporting personality has to go through three stages; arriving, adjusting, and consolidating. When you have 'arrived' in sport you get big headed. I defy anyone who has achieved something in a sport to avoid that completely. Some remain so. I went through it when I was shooting for Scotland at the age of sixteen or seventeen. It was inevitable. In 1959 and 1960 I won the British, Scottish, Irish, Welsh, and English Championships and the Coupe des Nations.

Then I got thrashed.

There is nothing more valuable. It was in 1960, on my twenty-first birthday, the last day of the trials for the British Olympic trap shooting team. Three of us were shooting it out for the two vacant places in the team. I had beaten the other guns consistently, but on one run of twenty-five clays I missed seven or eight. Unheard of, but there it was. It was a terrible blow to my ego, but it was the first time I had learned to face disappointment. It taught me to be philosophical about disappointments.

The incident taught Stewart a certain well-concealed humility. He never got into the habit of accepting defeat nobly and he won many more contests, but the writing was on the wall. He had tasted success in a limited way. Within a few years his interest in shooting waned and he looked for a new and bigger field to conquer.

He did not have far to look.

Aspiring motoring writer Eric Dymock on the forecourt of Stewart's of Dumbuck. The family home on right. Jaguar 3.8 Mark 2 carries Jimmy Stewart's BRDC badge. E-type on left is Dumbuck's demonstrator FSN1 young brother Jackie began racing.

Motor racing had fascinated him for years. Between the chastening failure to get into the Olympic team in 1960, and the winter of 1962, Jackie was still winning shooting competitions. It took him two years to lay down his competition gun. He employed the time with his first experiments in motor racing.

A wealthy customer of Dumbuck Garage, Barry Filer owned several cars which the garage prepared for local club races. Filer had chosen Dumbuck partly at least because with a former works racing driver in the family, they could be expected to know what they were doing. Friends of Filer's, mostly equally wealthy, drove the cars. Filer's family did not share his enthusiasm for racing driving and probably felt that the more his friends drove, the more likely Barry was to remain in one piece. Jackie acted as a sort of mechanic to the Filer stable at races, making sure the cars behaved suitably, and were immaculately turned out.

Filer's search for a driver eventually settled on young Jackie. Some of the wealthy friends had been unkind to the machinery, and rather on the basis that there was demonstrably driving talent in the family, and it seemed reasonable that if Stewart Minor was any good, the cars might earn themselves a laurel or two.

An early, ugly wooden-chassis Marcos, an Aston Martin DB4GT, an AC Ace, and then the E-Type Jaguar which was really the garage's demonstrator were the first cars Jackie raced. Barry Filer had no ambitions to set world champions off on an epoch-making motor racing career, yet that is just what he did.

Jackie clearly had talent. His first few races showed that. Early in 1962 came the decision that was to settle the destination of the 1969 World Driver's Championship, and who knows what more motor racing honours. Was Jackie Stewart to race or not?

He took the Jaguar, the Aston, and the Marcos to Oulton Park for a private test day. It was all a little bit of a lark, although the undertones were serious. Jackie drove from Scotland with three friends. They were a local golf champion and farmer from Bearsden, Jimmy Pirie; Glasgow motor trade executive and raconteur, Gordon Hunter; and Scotland's newest motoring journalist, Eric Dymock.

This was to be Jackie's moment of truth. He had decided that if he was able to reach competitive times at Oulton with any of the cars, he would take up racing seriously. To get some comparative times Jimmy Stewart drove the cars as well.

The stopwatch removed all doubt. Jackie lapped a track still dirty from winter at an impressive speed. With the E-Type, which had been only modestly tuned, he put up times as fast as a world class driver had done the previous autumn in a full race tuned lightweight E-Type. Jackie and his friends were convinced. It was an abandoned and carefree weekend. The pages of motor racing history seemed an unlikely destination for it at the time.

It was now a case of finding a drive or two. Jackie's ambition lay a little farther ahead than finding an enjoyable way of supplementing his income from the garage. If he ever felt he was World Championship material he kept the news to himself.

Perhaps someone who did recognise a champion was the great Scottish motor cyclist, and something of a hero to Jackie, Bob McIntyre. The first man to lap the Isle of Man TT course at 100 mph in 1957, McIntyre had taken an interest in Jackie. He had even contemplated taking up car racing himself and had already tried out the AC at Oulton Park. After his feat at the 'Golden Jubilee' TT where he won both the 500cc and 350cc TTs for Gilera, taking over from the injured Geoff Duke, McIntyre attacked world records. Gilera were going to retire from racing, and they went out with a record-breaking spree at Monza, some of which survive. McIntyre took the world's one-hour record with 141 miles, and this still stood in 1969 as a 350cc record.

In 1960 McIntyre joined Honda and lapped the TT course at 99.98 mph with a 250cc machine. He never won a World Championship, yet his riding was acknowledged to be championship class. He died from injuries received when he crashed a Norton in August 1962, on the eve, almost of his protege Jackie's breakthrough into front rank motor racing. His loss was keenly felt by Jackie for a long time.

Jackie was soon to marry his childhood sweetheart Helen McGregor. Her family's lack of enthusiasm at first caused little surprise. Jackie had not led what could be described as a sheltered life. In a relatively prim neighbourhood he was regarded as rather a racy young man with somewhat extravagant tastes, hardly ideal as a potential son-in-law. Helen's parents were not clairvoyant.

In truth, Jackie had been a little wild but like many of the other things he has made up his mind to do, settling down was something he did extremely effectively, and enjoyably with the initially shy, but pretty Helen. She remains an essential anchor for Jackie, resilient enough for his demanding way of life, bright, pert, and attractive. Helen is the perfect wife for Jackie, taking just the right amount of limelight, reacting to the unexpected in a practised way. Helen was right from the start.

Like any young couple they felt they could do with some money, and Jackie did no more than set out to employ his driving talent profitably. It was to show a good return.

Ecurie Ecosse began to show a keener interest in him, and he drove their ageing Cooper Monaco in sports car events. The famous Scottish team had somewhat fallen from grace since the palmy days in the middle fifties when they had two astonishing wins at Le Mans, against the might of works car opposition. They had never quite got over the surprise and were in the difficult position of never having been able to sustain the effort and expense of international racing thereafter. Yet sensibly David Murray, who ran the team decided their role must include the encouragement of young Scottish drivers.

They also encouraged young Scottish motoring journalists. Jackie Stewart joined them and put up some encouraging performances in the Cooper, and even contrived to gain some successes with their somewhat unmanageable Tojeiros, strangely prophetic mid-engined coupes, pioneers of a type of car which was to dominate the sports car races of the sixties.

But it was in the Ecurie Ecosse Cooper that Jackie showed he was a driver to be taken seriously.

2.

1964 and 1965

Up until Spa accident, June 1966

The destiny of the 1969 World Drivers Championship was decided earlier. Ken Tyrrell had discovered Jackie Stewart in the classic way that team managers discover racing drivers, or movie directors new film stars. A friend had said, 'You must see this brilliant youngster.' Lots of friends said that to Ken Tyrrell. It's a problem he has through his reputation for spotting new talent. 'I was not running a nursery for racing drivers,' he says. He was running a very successful team of racing cars. For 1964 he had two Cooper BMCs. His choice of Jackie Stewart to drive one, besides being one of the romances of motor racing, was the cornerstone of a World Championship six years hence. The partnership of Tyrrell, timber merchant from Surrey, and Stewart, Scottish racing driver was forged in the amateur atmosphere of Formula 3. Stewart and Tyrrell brought a professional approach.

Ken Tyrrell has probably been the most important influence in my racing career. Over the years, we have developed a great partnership similar to the one Jimmy Clark had with Colin Chapman although Ken's qualities are different. His strength lies mostly in having been entirely his own boss for so long. He has an independent nature which gives him a great ability for taking decisions, and in racing it is important to have someone who can take decisions without reference to a committee. There are numerous examples of people like this in racing because the nature of racing brings them out, and like people in the Alfred Neubauer (for many years Mercedes-Benz team chief) mould Ken's forcefulness, especially in moments of crisis, often takes people aback.

It is only within the last couple of years or so that I have been able to question his authority, not in a contradictory way, but as a complement to his experience. We work together by having a conversation, or a debate, not to argue out a compromise, just to see who is right.

For example, Ken taught me all about gear ratios when I drove for him in Formula 3. I came to his team a raw boy from the Highlands, unused to the professional approach in motor racing. Ken had the car set up for me and educated me in the selection of a high gear for slip-streaming circuits, or the most suitable intermediate gear for pulling away from an important comer. It was only when I returned to him in Formula 1 and demonstrated that I could analyse a car's behaviour to the satisfaction of experts like Iain Mills of Dunlop, or Bruno Morin, the Matra engineer in our tyre testing and development sessions, that he really believed I knew enough about it to discuss his decisions with him. We now have enough respect for each other to sit down and talk round a problem and this is an ideal situation.

His bluntness can sometimes be alarming until you get to know Ken. He does not cross people intentionally although he sometimes does so inadvertently, like the famous occasion at Mexico in 1969 when he threw Bernard Cahier out of the pit. Bernard is a fairly important man in motor racing, but Ken felt there were some people in the way and out they all went including Bernard. The incident had to be smoothed over afterwards because Bernard was understandably a bit ruffled about it, but Ken had decided the work of our chief mechanic Max Rutherford was being interrupted and that was sufficient reason to avoid a crowd.

I do not invariably agree with Ken. Our relationship would not have developed if I had because he is an argumentative man. He can be extremely uncompromising. Yet out of our debates the wisest solutions to problems usually emerge. The value of our partnership can be demonstrated by its success, and the strength of my friendship with, and admiration for Ken Tyrrell.

Of course, there is a gentler side to Ken which is seen to its best advantage in his ideal marriage. His concern for Norah when she was unwell, and their complete compatibility demonstrates what marriage is all about. They have a grown-up family and Norah certainly takes the prize for motor racing's best-looking grandmother. Her good nature and her great sense of humour have often been an asset to the team.

She must have had a sense of humour to have married Ken.

The only real drawback to working with Ken is his unerring aptitude for picking the worst hotels in the world. In our Formula 3 days we stayed in one for a race at Rouen which had naked light bulbs and plaster falling off the walls. What a miserable place it was, thank goodness Helen was not with me. I spent the entire night throwing rocks at the rats in the courtyard.

Things have improved a good deal, but Ken persists in staying at some awful places to this day.

In 1963 Tyrrell had had a young American driver, Tim Mayer, whose promise unhappily was never fulfilled. Mayer was killed during practice for a race in Australia in 1964. One day, when Ken was at Goodwood the subject of new drivers came up in conversation with Robin McKay the track manager. He had seen Stewart matching the sports car lap with a rather tired Ecurie Ecosse Cooper Monaco.

His advice to Tyrrell; 'Try out Stewart.'

Ken telephoned Dumbarton the same evening. Once again, the knowledge that there was driving talent in the family helped Jackie. Ken spoke to Jimmy Stewart. 'Do you know if he wants to become a Grand Prix driver? Is he serious?' Tyrrell asked. 'Or does he just do it for fun?' Jimmy said he reckoned young Jackie took his driving seriously, and Tyrrell invited him to Goodwood for a trial run in a new Formula 3 Cooper. Eric Dymock, now a London staff member at The Motor was there too, taking an opportunity to borrow Goodwood and secure pictures of a Porsche 1600SC he was testing.

It was Stewart's first drive in a single-seater racing car. 'I lectured him,' recalls Tyrrell. 'I said take it steady, we've got all day. Don't go too quickly.' Bruce McLaren was the Cooper works Formula 1 driver and had been recruited to come and give some comparative times to help judge the unknown Scot's performance. Stewart settled into the tiny single seater and set off. By his third lap he was equaling Bruce McLaren's time. Tyrrell did not believe a newcomer could get into a racing car, do this sort of time, and remain safe. He called Stewart in and gave him another lecture. Jackie went even faster.

It could have been a difficult situation. Bruce McLaren was an established Formula 1 star. Many another driver would have gone all temperamental. McLaren got back into the Cooper and lopped a second or two off his time. Stewart returned to the track and did the same. Ken stopped the session before it became a motor race, but not before everyone there, McLaren, Tyrrell, and John Cooper whose 'works' Formula 3 team Ken was really running, realised that the small, wiry driver they had seen that day was one of motor racing's great 'naturals'.

Ken Tyrrell's 1964 cars were Cooper BMCs which were driven by Jackie and Warwick Banks. It took all Tyrrell's diplomacy to satisfy Banks, who was a very capable and talented club driver, that his car was not slower than Stewart's. Jackie only failed to win two races during the entire year, and one of these was due to clutch failure on the warming-up lap. It was an astonishing performance.

I learned a great deal about Ken during this time. The team had to teach me, very patiently, all about professional motor racing without having me over-reach myself. In a race at Le Châtre in France, Alan Stait, who was our chief mechanic, worried greatly when the clutch broke and I had to start the race without it. There was one hairpin which was particularly difficult and I had to get round in a big old slide.

During the race I came up behind one particularly slow car and, unable to slip the clutch, rode up on his wheels and completely over him. The car came back to earth with a tremendous wallop just beside the pits and I found myself looking straight at Ken. He gazed for a moment in sheer astonishment but his appraisal of the situation was instantaneous. He made a lightning count of the wheels, found they added up to four, and in reply to my quizzical shrug, waved his arms and yelled across the road, 'GO ON.'

By the end of 1964 this almost unparalleled run of success could not be ignored. The 'boy wonder' legend had begun. Whatever Jackie Stewart did in motor racing seemed to succeed. He was never connected with anything that did not turn out sensationally successful. More surprisingly, the success seemed to take him unawares. His first Formula 3 triumph, a wet race at Snetterton where he led by several hundred yards at the end of the first lap, almost took his breath away. He kept looking round to see if he had jumped the start, or to find what was holding everyone else back. He could hardly believe it was his own driving.

Jackie Stewart remains a little bemused about his own innate, inborn skill at the wheel of a car. Confident, and self-assured in most ways, he knows he has a talent for

Jackie Stewart in the heavy H16 BRM airborne on one of the Nürburgring's bumps

Jackie Stewart takes a fast left-hander.

The H-16 at Spa. Under braking from 175 mph to 30 mph for the Hairpin. One of the BRM's wheels has locked.

driving, or reactions, or sense of balance, judgement, acuity of eyesight or whatever. Just as scientists identified the atom because it was the only logical explanation for the behaviour of materials, so Jackie Stewart knows that he must have something, some talent that makes him do what he does so well, but he appears uncertain as to what precisely it might be. This is not modesty; Jackie Stewart is not the modest sort. If he knew what it was, he would probably tell you, but he does not. This even troubles him because he occasionally seems afraid that he might wake up one morning and find it gone. So, he had better not bank on keeping whatever it is he doesn't know he has.

At the end of the almost unprecedented season with the Cooper, Jackie had offers from three Formula 1 teams. He had already driven for Team Lotus in the Rand Grand Prix.

I had just signed for BRM when I did my first Formula 1 race in a Lotus. Jimmy Clark had suggested I have a drive at a Team Lotus car during practice for the British Grand Prix in 1964. Colin agreed and I did a few laps at Brands. It must have been satisfactory because later in the year when Jimmy sustained a slipped disc throwing snowballs at Cortina, they offered me up as a substitute for the Team Lotus Formula 1 car and a Lotus Cortina in the Rand Grand Prix.

It was amusing in a way because here I was getting my first Formula 1 drive mostly for the experience. And there was a crowd of spectators expecting Jimmy Clark. They were very disappointed and of course I did not blame them, but it was important for me. Tony Rudd of BRM encouraged me to accept the drive and I did. The car was a brand new one which had been built for Jimmy and I took it off the line at the prescribed RPM and both drive shafts instantly broke. I won the second heat, but Graham Hill won the event on aggregate.

Chapman had been influenced by Ron Harris, who ran the Lotus works Formula 2 cars in 1964. Harris had given Jackie his most important race so far, the Formula 2 event on the Clermont-Ferrand track in south-west France.

A very significant point in my career came when Ron Harris asked me to drive at Clermont-Ferrand. Colin Chapman had later asked me to drive at Solitude in a Formula 1 event the same day. This was a matter of months only after I had first driven a single seater, yet Colin seemed at a loss to understand why I turned down an offer to drive a third car behind Jimmy Clark and Peter Arundel. But I felt I owed it to myself to go about my racing methodically. In any case Ron had asked me some time before Colin, and I was glad afterwards because the driver they did take on at Solitude crashed in the rain and took several cars off the road with him. If I had done that my career might never have recovered.

As it was, I came second to Denny Hulme at Clermont for a starting fee of £75 which barely covered my air fare. I learned a great deal; I was asked back by Ron and won my first Formula 2 race later in the season at Snetterton for him. And at Clermont I met and raced against, for the first time a great new Austrian driver. He came third and his name was Jochen Rindt.

Cooper and BRM were also interested in Jackie. Cooper seemed the natural place to go because they knew Jackie and he knew them; he would be amongst friends. But Cooper was about to lose Bruce McLaren, leaving to form his own racing organisation. John Cooper had had a road accident, and a team that had comparatively recently won two World Championships in quick succession was in disarray.

Lotus was tempting to join but clearly there might have been problems working with Colin Chapman, and at that time a Lotus number two driver could have a very thin time indeed. BRM on the other hand were riding the crest of a wave that had carried them to a World Championship in 1962 and kept them runners-up every year since. They had a brilliant 1½ litre V8 which, it seemed, was only beaten by Jimmy Clark's outstanding talent, so closely were the BRM and Lotus matched.

This was the last year of the 1½ litre Formula. The FIA, which makes the rules for motor racing, has the right to change the international Formula 1 as it is called, every four years. They arrange an appropriate set of regulations, or a formula to which racing cars of the leading category should be built. Usually this takes the form of a limitation on engine size. The top size between 1961 and the end of 1965 was 1½ litres with superchargers banned.

Cars had to be single seaters with exposed wheels, and run on 'pump' petrol, but otherwise there were few restrictions. For the following five years the FIA (Fédération International de l' Automobile) through its sporting sub-committee, the CSI (Commission Sportif Internationale, which has in turn a Technical Sub-

Committee) decided to change the rules again. This time, with the improvements which had taken place over the years in suspension and tyres, and the ability of cars to cope satisfactorily with power because they gripped the road better, they felt justified in doubling the permissible engine size. Previous changes had almost always been reductions on the grounds that engines always became more powerful, size for size, and to keep the performance within bounds it was necessary to reduce engine capacity. But the trend had been reversed and the 1966-70 Formula 1 was fixed at 3 litres with single seater cars stipulated as before, together with a minimum weight requirement to discourage lightening at the possible expense of safety.

The cars in World Championship Grands Prix were to comply with Formula 1, and the two other single-seater classes were Formula 2, fixed at 1,600 c.c. with engines loosely based on production cars, and Formula 3 which was fixed at 1,000 c.c. with engines based more strictly on production cars.

The proposal Jackie Stewart accepted was the one offered by BRM.

BRM had offered me no more money than Lotus. It was £4,000, but the difference was that Lotus had doubled and redoubled their figure to match BRM's, and I felt dubious about accepting something which they had had such difficulty arriving at. More important, BRM had promised me plenty of opportunities for test and development driving, which I felt was necessary to me. Again, BRM I felt would not push me too hard in my first year whereas Lotus might want me to justify myself quickly. Tony Rudd seemed prepared to let me find my own level.

Once again it was success all the way for Jackie Stewart. The 'Golden Boy' image was as bright as ever, brighter in fact as the season wore on. In his first race, the South African Grand Prix on January 1st, 1965, at East London he came sixth, scoring a first point in the World Championship. Back in Britain there was a race at Goodwood on Easter Monday where Jackie set up the joint lap record with Jim Clark, a record which will stand for all time since the circuit was closed soon after. Then he came second in the Race of Champions at Brands Hatch. Next was the Daily Express International Trophy at Silverstone which he won after a long race with John Surtees's Ferrari. At Monaco Stewart was third behind Graham Hill and Lorenzo Bandini's Ferrari. Then, at Spa in Belgium one very wet day in June 1965 he came second to his great friend and fellow-Scot, the very experienced Clark. In the French Grand Prix at Clermont-Ferrand he was again second to Clark. At Silverstone he gained the front row of the grid but only came fifth in the race which was another Clark triumph. In the Dutch Grand Prix, it was Clark and Stewart once again. At the Nürburgring he retired with bent suspension but at Monza the inevitable happened. Jackie Stewart won his first Grand Prix.

The win at Monza was a tremendous thing. I had no illusions about it, if a new driver is going to do well in a Grand Prix he will do well at Monza because although it calls for a special kind of driving it does not make great demands on ability, least not in the race. You need to be smooth and probably brave too, because you have to keep your foot 'in it' until the last instant at Monza or you lose yards to your opponents. I was delighted to have won the race, but it was just as well not to over-emphasise its importance.

Graham Hill in the other BRM and I were both racing to win at Monza, both going for the last corner with perhaps two laps to go when he got over on the grit near the edge of the track, just a fraction off line, but it was enough to hold him back and I went on to win the race.

I was worried in case I had been to blame, and I was not quite sure if everyone believed Graham's dismissal of the incident. They seemed to be thinking perhaps he was just being kind to the 'new boy', in what could have been a difficult situation.

Graham is one of the fairest men I know. Throughout the time we were at BRM he helped me, encouraged me in every way he possibly could and showed the utmost consideration. He was a great person to learn motor racing from and laid no blame against me for Monza in 1965. We were at a party in Milan that night when we saw the whole incident played back on a TV sports programme which showed that Graham had in fact gone a shade wide. This was seen by most of the people who mattered to me and showed them I was not trying to 'outfumble' a man for whom I still have a very high regard indeed.

Graham's strength of character showed through well in his 1968 Championship season. He had been in the team that had seen Jimmy Clark killed by what we all thought at first must be a mechanical failure but was later blamed on tyre deflation. Graham was still losing wheels and having suspensions break, yet he still raced, and raced more competitively and more determinedly than ever and I admired him more for that and his sheer professionalism than even his sense of fair play and his great ability.

He has a staying power that not only shows on the track when the chips are down, but it shows in his ability to go on racing year after year. He remains one of the best ambassadors motor racing has ever had. His bawdy after-dinner stories are told with a grace, elegance almost that makes them entirely acceptable in any company.

For as long as Graham Hill drives racing cars he will remain to be reckoned with.

The 'Golden Boy' failed to score further points during the 1965 Grand Prix season. But with one win, three seconds, one third, one fifth and one sixth giving him third place in the World Championship races in his first year of Grand Prix racing, Jackie Stewart was a motor racing phenomenon. Besides victory in the Silverstone International Trophy, a world-class but not a World Championship race, tenth at Le Mans with the Rover-BRM gas-turbine car with Graham Hill, his rate of successes throughout the sport was remarkable.

Early in 1966 BRM sent Stewart and Hill to the Tasman Series of races, their 1965 Grand Prix cars with the V8 engines stretched to 2 litres. Richard Attwood deputised in one race for Hill and won it, Hill won two races, and Jackie Stewart four, leaving only one to Jim Clark in an admittedly underpowered 2½ litre Lotus Climax. BRM and Stewart returned victorious for the first 3 litre season of Grand Prix races in Europe.

It began in fine style. Still with the 2 litre car, Stewart won the Monaco Grand Prix from Lorenzo Bandini, with Graham Hill third and American Bob Bondurant fourth in another BRM. At Indianapolis Stewart drove a Lola and led from the 147th to the 192nd of the 200 laps before retiring when a scavenge pump failed. With almost a lap in hand it was an almost unprecedented performance in the annals of the 500-mile classic. Nothing, it seemed, could stop sweeping the 26-year-old dramatically to the forefront of international motor racing alongside the great Clark. The conclusion that here was one of the world's greatest drivers in the making was now inescapable. His career seemed unstoppable because like Clark's, although it had not been completely accident-free, he had never been seriously hurt in a racing car.

At Spa, in Belgium on June 12, 1966, it all very nearly came to a sudden and tragic end. At the time, such was the impetus of his successes that it seemed nothing more than a check in his career. Yet it was two long years before Jackie Stewart was ever to win a Grand Prix again. Two long years in which to prepare himself for his next bid for the World Championship. The preparation as a racing driver was complete. Failure, it is said, is good for character-building. The next two years Jackie Stewart used to build character and prepare, plan, and with Ken Tyrrell create a new racing organisation which would make him the 1969 Champion Driver of the World.

3.

Remainder of 1966, 1967

The Spa catastrophe was one of motor racing's most famous accidents, and one with far-reaching consequences not only for the tremendously fast Spa circuit, but also for motor racing as a whole. It highlighted a number of requirements needed to make it safer and set two men off on a crusade to make sure that something was done about it. They were Jackie Stewart and Louis Stanley.

It was the second race that season in which most of the field had been involved in a multiple pile-up on the first lap: at Indianapolis, chaos had erupted as the rolling start got under way in clouds of smoke and a cascade of detached wheels before the crowded grandstands. Fortunately, injuries were superficial. Now, at Spa, on the fastest road racing circuit in the world sixteen cars set off along the treacherous 8¾ mile ribbon of smooth tarmac in the Belgian Ardennes.

It was dry at the start, but on the other side of the circuit, 4 miles away, the road was awash after a heavy shower of rain. Jo Bonnier (Cooper-Maserati), Mike Spence (Lotus BRM), Denny Hulme (Brabham Climax), and Jo Siffert (Cooper Maserati) all spun off the track at Malmedy. Further down the road, on the Masta Curve, a 150-mph bend, the BRMs of Bob Boudurant, Graham Hill, and Jackie Stewart all went off. Hill found Stewart half-conscious, trapped in the car which had hit a post sideways breaking open the brimming fuel tanks, soaking the driver in petrol.

Stewart, the only driver injured, had a painful journey to hospital at Verviers. The ambulance driver lost his way. The agonizing half hour when he lay pinned in the car drenched in fuel with a broken shoulder, a cracked rib, and painful internal bruising was the longest of his life. The rain that day would not have put out the fire which would have consumed him. The memory must be an effective answer to the critics of his, and Louis Stanley's efforts to promote safety in motor racing.

Louis Stanley is an extraordinary man. He has many talents and some failings, not all of which are obvious to him. He writes a very amusing book, takes terrible pictures, and can be diplomatic or not depending on the circumstances.

In the back of the ambulance to Verviers after the Spa accident, Louis was sitting on a chair at the bottom of the bed, and I was suffering from shock and the pain of the injuries. Louis is a big man, a daunting character in many ways with an imperious manner and I had always deferentially called him Mr Stanley when he was there, and like everyone else, Big Lou when he was not.

I was lapsing in and out of consciousness and in my muddled way felt this was no time to stand on ceremony. 'Lewis', I enquired, 'Is Helen all right?' Or, 'Lewis, where are we going?' 'Lewis, would you do this?' And 'Lewis, would you do that?' He was being very patient and comforting me as best as he could, but his dignity could stand 'Lewis' no longer. Eventually, he leaned over me and said 'Stewart! If you insist on calling me by my Christian name, call me Louie.'

Only he could think of anything like that in such circumstances.

He is a great man in many ways and his advocacy of the Grand Prix Medical Service is the result of finding out at first-hand what a shambles aid for injured drivers can often be. His motives are perfectly sincere. His biggest shortcoming is that he tends to take things too far and instead of curtailing an argument when he has won, he gets carried away with himself. This is a pity because many of the points he makes are very valid if only he would stop overstating his case. He often fails to recognize this, and it is difficult to point it out to him when really his heart is in what he does.

Returning to the pre-Spa situation in which Jackie Stewart found himself we have this new young driver rising, it seemed, to the peak of his performance. He had had a sensational 1965 debut in Formula 1. He had won the Tasman Championship, nearly won Indianapolis where, remember, Europeans had never been very competitive and here he was very nearly winning at his first attempt. He had won Monaco and was facing up to the strong Honda challenge in Formula 2 with a great deal of promise.

Matra first cropped up when Ken came back from the party after the 1965 French Formula 2 Championship. We had been running a Cooper BRM and a Cooper Cosworth with very little success. Someone had suggested he run Matra cars in Formula 2 next season and Ken reckoned it might be worthwhile testing them. We had been thinking about a Lola or a Brabham or some make that we knew, and I really felt a bit dubious about anything else. 'What sort of car's this?' I said. 'It's a French car.' Well, this spelt trouble to me immediately. I couldn't imagine why Ken wanted a French car unless as a result of a particularly good evening in Paris and somebody giving him a good line of chat. However, he was persistent and told me all about the impressive Matra record in Formula 3. We decided to have a test session.

Ken lent them an engine to put into a Matra chassis to try at Goodwood. It seemed particularly successful in transmitting its power to the road, which is important in a racing car; it means more than just having a good grip of the road. It means that coming out of comers you can accelerate a fraction sooner, a little more emphatically and you will not lose power in wheelspin, or with the tail flicking out. The designers had contrived to improve the traction between the rear tyres and the road surface by building in just the right amount of chassis stiffness, just the right suspension geometry to get the right answer. The car was not perfect. It understeered, or ran wide on comers, but I felt sure this was a question of adjustment rather than a basic shortcoming.

The car itself was very much a rush job, a Formula 3 with a Formula 2 engine, but it was vital to get it on test as soon as possible because I had to get off to the Tasman Series and a decision before then was essential. I went away feeling enthusiastic about Matra and Ken prepared to make some sort of arrangement with them for Formula 2 in 1966.

Jackie went off to the Tasman Series, leaving the whole deal in Ken's capable hands. There was a snag when he found that the French firm did not keep its bargain to give Tyrrell exclusive use of a Matra chassis for the season. They sold one to John Coombs for Graham Hill to drive, whereas Jackie felt that if the Tyrrell Racing Organisation was going to take the risk of running this little-known make of car, with all the development work it was going to demand, then they should have a year of freedom with it. As it happened Hill didn't much like his Matra and subsequently changed it.

Jack Brabham and Denny Hulme had Brabham Hondas winning just about everything that year. Our first race was on Easter Monday at Goodwood, and I kept up with them until I ran over the kerb at the Chicane and broke the throttle linkage where it projected through the floor. The kerb actually knocked the head off a bolt and therefore allowed the accelerator pedal to fall off in the full throttle position and drop behind the brake pedal. This meant that I entered St Mary's with the car at full throttle and no way of putting on the brakes, so I switched off and headed straight for the infield. I had no choice in the matter as it happened.

Jacky Ickx had joined us in the team, and I took over his car for the remainder of that race and kept station with the Hondas again. It showed that the car was competitive, and this was confirmed at Barcelona where we took two laps off the Brabhams in the rain until the battery went flat. At this time everybody was using the same sort of tyres. We had no super-tweaky rain tyre with channels and suchlike as we developed later.

It was an indifferent start to the season, but we were building up a friendship, an association with Matra engineers and with people like Jean-Luc Lagardere its Director General. The season could have been more successful. I felt the car was competitive but then I had my accident in Belgium and that kept me out of several races. We were using a BRM engine as well as the Ford engine and that brought problems, but the team was being forged and that was what mattered.

What a contrast at the start of this year compared with 1966. Jackie had physically recovered from the accident, but it had undoubtedly dawned on him that motor racing was dangerous. The Matra was good, but not yet completely convincing, and the BRM had been extremely unsatisfactory. This was the trough, a despondent period when motor racing was a very discouraging business for him.

BRM unfortunately just were not competitive. They had been trying to make the new H16 engine work and found that it did not. I had concentrated on driving the V8, now enlarged to 2.2 litres to see what we could salvage in some of the races. I got back behind the wheel for the British Grand Prix after the Spa accident but the engine broke after 17 laps. At Holland we managed fourth,

The 1968 South African Grand Prix at Kyalami.

two laps adrift. In Germany, on a wet and miserable Nürburgring we were fifth. At Monza with the H16 we went out with a fuel leak. In America it was the engine after 53 laps and in Mexico an oil leak after 26, both with the H16. Graham had had no better luck. It was all rather saddening, and we had both almost decided to leave the team. Colin Chapman approached us individually and Graham accepted an offer to join Lotus for 1967 which also gave him a drive at Indianapolis where he had won in 1966.

I agreed to remain with BRM for another year and also with Dunlop. Lotus were a Firestone contracted team. It was quite a good arrangement so far as I was concerned. I was number one driver with no formally arranged number two, but it was agreed that Mike Spence, Piers Courage, Dick Attwood or Chris Irwin would share in the other cars.

The first race of the 1967 season was the South African Grand Prix which Pedro Rodriguez won, and where my H16 engine fell apart at the end of the straight after only three laps. I did the Tasman Championship once again for BRM between flying back to South Africa to do tyre testing, losing the Tasman title through continual transmission failures despite wins in the New Zealand Grand Prix at Pukekohe and the Australian Grand Prix at Warwick Farm. About the only thing I could do anything about was tyres.

It had to be made quite clear to Dunlop that I felt they were being left behind by Firestone and Goodyear. I went a long way to make things plain to them in fact, very early in 1967. I had been to Johannesburg to do some testing for Dunlop and BRM, they both needed development and flew back to England and sat down with the directors at Fort Dunlop for lunch. The Directors of Research and the Tyre Division were there; it was a pretty big meeting.

Unfortunately, I was very harsh on them and said I did not think the British company had any clue at all about what was going on internationally in racing. I felt they did not have a hope of catching the Americans so much so that Harry Badger, Director of Development, Tyres, left the table saying that since Mr Stewart felt so strongly about Dunlop, then perhaps he (Badger) had better leave and get on with his work. It was a bit embarrassing all round. He later became one of the men responsible for the racing effort at Dunlop and a very close friend. At the time I am sure he thought I was being impertinent but really, it was all plain fact. Dunlop just weren't in the business, and it took them another year before they were. But something must have struck a chord somewhere because they began to support their Racing Division very strongly.

We had a new Matra which was very different from the old one. The chassis had different suspension mounting points, Formula 2 was now 1600 cc and there was an increase in fuel capacity, so it felt quite new. With the bigger engine this quality of being able to use all the power became even more important.

We had been doing a lot of testing, and while I never feel I have directly influenced the design or layout of any racing car, we certainly had been giving the Matra designers a lot of our personal reactions to the car. These designers looked at motor racing very thoroughly and found out what was required of a racing car and exactly what its purpose was. They did a lot of research aimed simply at keeping the wheels hard on the ground at every possible moment, in every sort of condition of bump and rebound. I could tell whether they were achieving useful results but left the engineering to them.

They managed this pretty well in 1967 because we had a good Formula 2 car. We were however behind the Firestones and Goodyears and in the early part of the season we were very short of successes. The BRM situation in Formula 1 was almost as bad. I had finished second at Spa when I maybe could have won. The car started to fall out of gear and Dan Gurney caught up and passed me.

The 1967 record was to say the least disappointing in Formula 1. At Monaco Stewart retired the V8 BRM while in the lead when the crown wheel failed. At the famous Zandvoort race where the Ford Cosworth V8 made its debut and won, Stewart retired the H16 after 51 laps with brake trouble. Then came the encouraging performance at Spa, and third in the French Grand Prix on the twisty Bugatti circuit at Le Mans with only the V8 because it somehow matched the track. At Silverstone the H16 went out with transmission trouble, and in Germany it was the crown wheel again. In Canada Stewart's H16 was one of two to retire with sand in the vulnerable throttle slides. At Monza the engine let him down, at Watkins Glen the fuel injection drive broke. In the final race at Mexico, he had to retire yet again with vibration problems in the H16. The World Championship score was a lowly 10 points, bringing him into ninth position.

In Formula 2 Jochen Rindt emerged as the man to beat. In 1967 he won nine of the 15 races he entered and was second in four others. He won both the British and French Formula 2 Championships.

During this time Jochen was a bit of an enigma. He didn't mix very much; he has mellowed a great deal over the last two years or so. He was a very determined young man with very set ideas. He did not come and go very much with anybody, was a bit unyielding and this showed in his racing. Jochen had an almost incredible amount of natural talent which he had shown throughout his career. He drove in Formula 2 with enormous verve and obvious pleasure, but in a wild sort of way without somehow ever arriving at the accident. He seemed to have a flair for getting the car into apparently ridiculous positions, crazy angles as he slid through the corners, and yet he always got it back into shape and he remained the man to beat, beyond doubt.

Our big breakthrough in 1967 came undoubtedly with the introduction of the Dunlop 970 compound. By the end of the season, we were back amongst the front runners in Formula 2 and in fact won four major races in the latter part of the year. The 970 was originally for use in the rain. They thought it would be too soft for the dry, it was expected to wear quickly. But we used it, and it played a great part in our success then and subsequently. It was so good in fact that up till the end of 1969 we were never able to improve on it.

You could say it all really started to happen at Karlskoga, the Formula 2 Swedish Grand Prix in 1967. Jochen and I had almost identical times in practice and had a great race. We were very little apart at the finish, fortunately with me in front. Then I won the Mediterranean Grand Prix at Enna, always a bit of a lottery, and the Formula 2 section of the Oulton Park Gold Cup race. Then I was second at Brands Hatch behind Jochen. The last major race of the season was at Albi, and I won that too. We really felt that we were beginning to see the light. Jacky Ickx was with the team this year and he won the European Championship for nongraded drivers which pleased us all greatly.

It seemed that the support the Dunlop directors were giving their racing people was beginning to bear fruit. We tried the new tyre on the BRM as well, but the car was too big and too heavy to ever gain a real advantage from it. Alec Meskell had been the tyre technician most closely connected with the track development of the 970 and he was 'our' tyre man. We worked up a very good relationship with Alec and also with Iain Mills, the Dunlop racing tyre designer. We remained closely involved with them throughout 1968 and the Championship year of 1969.

Dunlop all of a sudden realised that these men had produced a tyre for them that was going to be very big in motor racing.

I first met Iain Mills in the back of the transporter in 1967 when we were engaged in a test programme with the H16 BRM. He was to become a very colourful member of the team, with his deerstalker and rather rotund figure bouncing along taking tyre temperatures and generally supervising the behaviour of the products he had designed.

Jacky Ickx was a good team member. His English was steadily improving, it had been almost non-existent when he came into the team but gradually it got better and better. Ford were very keen to have him, he had been a Ford boy from the start and had had a lot of help from Ford Belgium.

One curious aspect of Jacky Ickx's performances in his early days with Ken Tyrrell's Formula 2 cars was his consistent refusal to give his best when Stewart was present. When the responsibility was entirely on his own shoulders he always did very well, but race records of the time indicate that his lap speeds were down on Stewart's by a second, or a second and a half. Yet he was invariably equal to exactly the same opponents when Stewart was racing elsewhere.

When he came to Brands Hatch to test the first 1,600cc. Cosworth-engined Formula 2 cars he confided to Ken Tyrrell that they felt very quick, and he would need time to get familiar with their performance. Yet he was always a brilliant performer, able to cope with any opposition and push the car to lap record-breaking drives, provided he was chief team driver. Only when Stewart was present did he seem to hold something back.

Stewart probably wishes he still did.

Another development which might have changed the course of events in 1968 and 1969 was an approach during 1967 for me to drive for Ferrari. Keith Ballisat of Shell had been very keen to get me to do so but I did not much care for Ferrari's way of working with drivers. In particular I had heard about him pushing drivers to be competitive with each other within the team and rather upsetting the emotional side of motor racing.

I went down to Maranello in June very unwillingly, but I must admit to being very impressed with the place. The discussions with Mr Ferrari were only exploratory at the time; I was interested in making a move because of my misfortunes with BRM, and Ferrari said he would like me to drive his cars but nothing much was decided on that visit.

Next time I saw them was just before Enna, and Franco Gozzi and Franco Lini who was then the Ferrari team manager were involved in the discussions. Mr Ferrari met me at the gate this time, which made me feel he thought the visit fairly important, and we went into long discussions at the little restaurant across the road where I gather most of Ferrari's business happens.

We talked finance, in fact it was completely agreed financially, and Ferrari seemed a superb organisation for making racing cars, just what I was looking for. But I reckoned I needed a contract with Ferrari, so I passed the arrangement we had worked out over to my lawyers.

Next thing I heard was that a Ferrari drive had been offered to Jacky Ickx because Jackie Stewart had asked for too much money and the old man would take on Ickx if he could have Ickx's word immediately.

Imagine how I felt. I had been apprehensive about joining Ferrari, but I had shaken hands on an agreement to carry on negotiations and possibly drive a Ferrari the following year. I had been apprehensive about just this sort of thing, and I immediately thought, 'This is it - finished.' I telephoned Keith Ballisat and told him the deal was off. He tried to change my mind, but I said I simply could not deal with Mr Ferrari. He said, 'Well, maybe Mr Ferrari did not know about it.' Mr Ferrari denied all knowledge, but anyway I did not change my mind.

Ken Tyrrell had already said that he was interested in having a Formula 1 team. He reckoned that if I was going to be successful in Grands Prix then I had to have a Ford Cosworth DFV engine. I did not see that he had any hope at all of putting the deal together, because he needed money, and he needed all sorts of other things. He thought that Matra would be keen to make a Formula 1 chassis for him if he could supply the engines because it was not going to be much different from Formula 2.

He managed to get all this together by around Monza, at which time I had finally said no to Ferrari. Mr Ferrari in the meantime had got very upset and anti-Jackie Stewart and said I was only interested in money and had gone to Ford because they had paid me off, which was not true. In fact, I did not even have a deal at the time. Talks with BRM were continuing because they had decided to make a V12, and they offered me very good money. But by this time, I needed a race winning car more than anything else and I finally agreed to go along with Ken Tyrrell. We had meetings with Dunlop to have their complete association with us, as well as the services of their tyre development team. Matra were giving us trackside help in the form of a chassis designer and a lot more besides.

I liked Ken and had confidence in his management, and once again it was a very satisfactory arrangement financially. It seemed the logical thing to do at the time; looking back I suppose it was quite courageous of us all to undertake the Matra project. The engine had been proved, the chassis seemed competitive, and so, I felt, was I. The team manager and the mechanics were good, and we had all worked together before. Yet it was done with a feeling of hope rather than an expectation of winning the World Championship.

4.

The 1968 season

By the beginning of 1968 Jackie Stewart was back on the Championship trail. With the despondent period from the autumn of 1966 until his Karlskoga win behind him, and an end, he felt, to the miserable succession of DNFs in his last two years with BRM, the Matra Formula I venture went ahead. Jackie was again bent on a World Championship even though he hardly dared hope that this was the way to go about it.

The great win of 1968; Jackie Stewart in the rain at the German Grand Prix.

The whole deal was arranged so quickly that we had a car ready for the South African Grand Prix on 1st January 1968, which was pretty remarkable. 'Ready' is perhaps an exaggeration, it looked like something you would use on a farm. It was unpainted, and not much more than the Formula 2 car, the MS 8 with extra tanks to carry enough fuel for a Formula 1 race. It was known as the MS 9 and we had had hardly any opportunity to do any testing on it. One damp December lunch time I had driven it at Montlhery just outside Paris, for a few laps. As a measure of our confidence, we had also taken out a Formula 2 car with Jean-Pierre Beltoise to drive it.

The car was promising in practice, qualifying third on the front row of the grid, so we knew that we were competitive.

Stewart was so competitive that he led the first lap of the race from Jim Clark's Lotus. Clark overtook and went on to win his 25th and sadly, his last Grand Prix. Graham Hill in the other Lotus passed Stewart on lap 28 and the hastily cobbled Matra ran third until lap 44, just over half distance when the Ford Cosworth engine broke a connecting rod. Ken Tyrrell's first major bill in Grand Prix racing was £1,700 for an engine rebuild. Hill came second behind Clark, with Rindt in his first Brabham drive third, Amon fourth in a Ferrari one lap behind. Denny Hulme in his first race for McLaren was fifth, also one lap behind.

Lotus were undoubtedly going to be the keenest opposition in 1968. On 1st January in South Africa, they were undoubtedly the most formidable team on the grid, and they proved it in the race. Here was a very, very good team; Colin Chapman with a fine chassis, and the most competitive engine, the Ford engine that had already been proved in 1967 and won four Grands Prix. The 1968 season was made for Chapman. He had sponsorship, he had the cars and drivers, he had arranged his whole business very, very well indeed. On the starting grid of the South African Grand Prix, he had the first and second fastest time. Lotus had Jimmy who doesn't need any additional praise from me. He was the complete Grand Prix driver. He was the fastest driver sitting on that grid. Graham Hill was the most determined and the driver who was the most likely to win there if Jim Clark didn't. To have this sort of experience and determination in a team is a colossal asset. No team had ever been in such a good position at the start of any racing season.

Disaster struck, not just for Team Lotus but for everybody in motor racing when Jimmy died in April. Graham was affected by this. I suppose he would deny it, but he was not driving at his best afterwards. His car was one of the best in the Grand Prix field of 1968, but its failures had affected Graham's confidence as I believe they would have affected almost anyone's. It must have taken a lot of sheer bravery to drive it as competitively as he did and ultimately win the World Championship with it.

Lotus had to take on Jackie Oliver as number two driver. Jackie was completely new, and it was a big responsibility for a youngster to come into such an important team, particularly when Lotus's enormous prospects for the season seemed destroyed in the tragedy of Jim Clark. Ferrari had Chris Amon, fourth in South Africa and a very talented driver. They also had Jacky lckx, who looked like being very good indeed. But with their hill climb, their Formula 2, their prototypes, and their Formula 1 cars they were clearly trying to do too much. You could never discount them, but they were using a V12, and it had been proved fairly conclusively that a V8 was the engine to beat.

McLaren, still benefiting from the Robin Herd-designed car, looked very competitive. It was very good looking until they brought out a side tank affair at the Spanish Grand Prix which never turned out so well. Denny Hulme was still World Champion and there was also Bruce - no one really knew about Bruce because while he was a very good Grand Prix driver, he was not considered to be a very fast Grand Prix driver. Denny was always the more likely of the pair to be ahead at the end of the race. Denny had taken the unusual step of leaving Brabham right after his World Championship and joining McLaren.

Brabham had taken on Jochen Rindt who had been unable to leave Cooper due to a contractual problem. He had made an unfortunate choice joining Cooper in the first place for 1965 because he had signed a three-year contract which seemed unsatisfactory, and he was stuck with a rather uncompetitive car. He had shown that he was a very skilled driver and now chose to go with Brabham. He felt that Brabhams had just won two Championships, it was a good handling car (he drove a Brabham successfully in Formula 2) and he was very happy indeed with the arrangement. Yet I was surprised that he went there. He had seen the power of the Ford Cosworth V8, he was going to use the Repco engine which he knew was not as powerful and he had no real guarantee that the four overhead camshaft version under development would be much better.

The engine in fact proved to be overstretched. It had reached the limit of its development. Jochen was going to be good on some circuits but certainly handicapped because his engine was not as good as the Ford. He just did not have the machinery to do the job and the same went for the incredible Jack Brabham.

BRM were pinning their hopes on the V12 and started off looking very good. They had Mike Spence and Pedro Rodriguez driving and Mike had been doing a lot of development work and been a great help to the team because he was taking a very big personal interest. He did very well in the Race of Champions and put up race winning performances. His driving was getting better as he matured, and he was just the man BRM needed at this juncture. Everyone was getting quite excited about Mike.

Then, with Jimmy's accident and Parnelli Jones's withdrawal from Indianapolis, Mike went there to drive for Andy Granatelli's STP team and Colin Chapman. During practice Mike hit the wall that lines the track and received head injuries from which he died the same night. It was really tragic that his life should have been taken in those circumstances. He was becoming a strong force to be reckoned with in Grand Prix racing and his loss to BRM was incalculable.

BRM carried on with Pedro, but they didn't seem to have the confidence in him that they had had in Mike. Cooper had just lost Jochen. They had been in decline for some time and now had this very uncompetitive chassis, Maserati and later BRM engines, which were equally unsatisfactory. They had Lodovico Scarfiotti, who was to be another great loss before the season was a few months old. Lodovico was a great personality, a great gentleman, a great hill climber and talented sports car driver - he was certainly Formula 1 calibre.

A plastic moulding held Stewart's arm together during most of the 1968 season.

Stewart and Ken Tyrrell at Nürburgring.

Graham Hill about to win the World Championship of 1968.

The Matra MS 10 locks a wheel approaching the Spa hairpin.

Honda had John Surtees and were certainly doing their best to be competitive. Unfortunately, John has been finding difficulty over the years getting a team that would either stand the pace of his demands or come up with machinery good enough to win races. This seems to have dogged him ever since his disagreement with and departure from Ferrari in 1966. He has never been with a successful team since, and in fact some teams seem to have disintegrated with him because he is so demanding. Yet he shows more dedication to the sport than any other driver. He deserves more success.

Rob Walker is one of motor racing's 'greats'. He has been competing for around 34 years in Grand Prix racing. Not only that but he has taken part in every British Grand Prix ever run. Rob's profession on his passport is said to be 'gentleman' which he really is. He is respected and liked throughout motor racing for his manners and his good humour. He seems to have lost none of his enthusiasm over the years and he really is very, very good for motor racing. Jo Siffert, who drove Rob's car became a very proficient Grand Prix driver. He has had wonderful success with Porsches in sports car racing but his association with Rob Walker must have been one of the best things that ever happened to him.

The opposition looked formidable. But Lotus no longer had the monopoly of the Ford engine. McLaren had it and so had we. Brabham was always menacing with Jochen and Jack in the team. The Honda was to some extent an unknown quantity, but they had won the last 1½ litre Grand Prix in their first year in Formula 1 and after Surtees's great win at Monza you never knew what they could come up with. Neither BRM nor Ferrari could be entirely discounted.

After the encouraging performance at Kyalami the team relaxed only briefly. They went back to Europe to complete the transition from MS 9, really a development of the Formula 2 car, to the MS 10 in time for the opening event of the European season, the Race of Champions at Brands Hatch. BRM had its new V12 engined cars here with monocoques based on a design by Len Terry. The McLaren Ford resembled the Lotus by having the engine fixed rigidly to the bulkhead behind the driver as a stressed part of the frame. There was also a· new Cooper with a BRM engine along the lines of the 'flat' Cooper-Maserati which appeared in 1967.

Matra-Ford MS10.01 had been built in February. The Ford-Cosworth engine had not been used to carry the rear suspension. Instead, there was a small tubular sub-frame bolted to the bulkhead behind the cockpit and running rearwards to a steel frame enclosing the engine. There was a Hewland gearbox, Lucas electronic ignition and fuel injection, and Autolite spark plugs. The monocoque was made of aluminium and the suspension was conventional for Grand Prix cars with wishbones and outboard coil spring damper units at the front, and two long trailing arms at the rear. Nose and driver's seat were reinforced glass fibre with an unusually solid double tube roll-over bar. As a fire prevention device, a control near the driver's head led to the battery master switch at the rear of the car.

At the Race of Champions, Stewart finished sixth in the very new car, one lap in arrears, after a pit stop to fix his pedal pivot arrangements because the brake and the clutch were fouling each other. The race was won by Bruce McLaren and was notable for a good showing by the new BRMs. Stewart again showed the Matra was competitive, being third fastest in practice against the 1968 works cars except the absent Honda, Eagle, Brabham and the official Matra V12 which had just been announced.

Matra International did not compete in the next race, the Daily Express Silverstone, again won by a McLaren, driven this time by Denny Hulme. The next Grand Prix was May, the Spanish at Jarama, but only after another interruption in Stewart's career.

Jackie had driven Ken Tyrrell's Formula 3 Coopers in 1964. In 1965 he signed with BRM in Formula 1 and drove for Ken Tyrrell again with Coopers uprated to Formula 2. In 1966 he was again with BRM, had his Spa accident and the unsatisfactory season with Tyrrell and the Formula 2 Matras. In 1967 he remained with BRM and had a second year with Matra, now with the 1,600cc Cosworth engine in Formula 2, culminating in four wins at the end of the season which showed Dunlop they were on to something.

Now, in 1968 Stewart had moved into Formula 1 with the Tyrrell Matra team, known as Matra International, and obviously wanted to continue with Matra in Formula 2 as well. The difficulty was that Tyrrell had his hands full. John Coombs was keen to be involved however, and he took over the Formula 2 Matra operation at the beginning of 1968.

My first experience with John Coombs, after reading about him when people like Graham Hill, Jack Sears and Roy Salvadori drove his cars, was in 1964. He had a lightweight E-type that he asked me to try out at Silverstone. This was important for me because John Coombs is a very big name in motor racing, and this really seemed like the big time. Apparently, the idea had come from FRW (Lofty) England of Jaguar cars. We at Dumbuck were Jaguar dealers, and of course so was Coombs at Guildford.

I went to Silverstone and met Noddy Coombs, everyone calls him Noddy - it seemed to fit. He has bright orange hair, and he is a very sarcastic little man, really quite pompous until you get to know him. But after you do, he is one of the most amusing men you could ever wish to know. He is one of the most reliable and one of the most genuine people in racing. A great fusser and terribly nervous.

He was a very good team manager in 1968 except that he got very excited, he was absolutely a bundle of nerves. He could eat nothing the morning of a race, would hardly talk to you. He kept telephoning to see if you were all right and I suppose we played a bit on John's nervousness. He walked up and down the pits all the time eating sweets.

John and Ken negotiated all the starting money arrangements and all the day-to-day running was done by John. Ken was responsible to Matra for the operation, but it was John's mechanics, Roland Law and his team, who carried out work on the car and transported it. The car was kept between John Coombs's racing department at Guildford and taken to Paris whenever any major work was needed. Johnny Servoz-Gavin was with us in the team.

Things looked encouraging for a time. We had had a promising beginning in South Africa in Formula 1 and won three races out of four starts in Formula 2, then went back to Jarama for the next Formula 2 race on the weekend of the 27th/28th of April. I had established pole position on the grid and thought I had the whole thing tied up as much as you can think that before a race. Then I took the car out to check something just before finishing practice. I made what seemed a minor error of judgement on the right-hand corner behind the pits, locked a wheel and went straight into a wire mesh fence. It was a tight corner, so my right hand was underneath my left on the spoke of the steering wheel which jerked when the front wheels hit a post. This twisted my wrist. I knew I had hurt it, but never imagined the consequences. It was not painful, just a dull ache and I walked back to the pits, the car was hardly damaged at all. It was in no way a serious accident.

As we drove into Madrid later, it began to get really sore, and I decided to have it X-rayed just to be on the safe side. There was no sign of a fracture, but the surgeon said, 'I think you've got a broken scaphoid.' I did not know what he meant, and I said, 'It would show on the X-ray.'

'No,' he said, 'it would take two or three weeks to show on the X-ray.'

So, I went off to the hotel and suffered the most excrutiating pain the whole night; I have never felt so sorry for myself. By morning the wrist had swollen and there was no hope of me driving a racing car that day. The surgeon said, 'I told you so,' put my arm in plaster saying it was better this way and I turned up at the track like that much to the glee of Rindt and company. Other racing drivers can sometimes be unsympathetic.

This was the start of lengthy consultations with doctor after doctor, X-ray after X-ray. Always there was the same verdict. 'No, it won't show on the X-ray yet, but we think you have a broken scaphoid.' Jackie had to cancel his drive at Indianapolis. More consultations all indicated the same thing. Jackie refused to believe it until one doctor showed him, with a multi-magnifying X-ray machine in Chicago, a shadow on the bone. Twenty weeks in plaster was the best verdict he ever obtained.

The Spanish Grand Prix came and went in May. Team Lotus, bereft of Jim Clark won it with Graham Hill. Jean Pierre Beltoise took over Jackie's MS 10 and had led until a fourpenny washer came undone, eventually finishing fifth. Jackie went to Monaco but still could not drive. This time Jean-Pierre was in the V12 Matra and Johnny ServozGavin took over Jackie's car, made a sensational start but clouted the wall at the chicane putting the car out of the race.

By Monaco I was feeling a bit upset. Graham had now won two of the three races and had a total of 24 points before I had gained a single one. We knew the car was a match for anyone after Jean-Pierre's and Johnny's performances, making matters worse for me having to stand and watch. It was just as bad for Ken. My big lecture to Servoz before Monaco had not been sufficient to restrain him. He is a good driver but just had not enough experience. I had suggested that Richard Attwood be tried in the car. He was experienced and he knew Monaco, but because of the French connection Ken chose Servoz. As it happened, Richard put up a very good show in the BRM, so much in fact that he was hailed as a sort of new Mike Hawthorn afterwards.

Monte Carlo demands a very special sort of start. The track is slippery for the first few laps. I told Servoz this before the race with Jabby Crombac interpreting just to make sure there was no misunderstanding, but he got a bit excited. It was a French crowd and he had got on to the front row of the grid - it was all very understandable. I spun the car my first time at Monte Carlo, so it had been done before. But Johnny is a very nice young man, and it helped him to realise that he must take his motor racing more seriously and shed his playboy image before he was going to win any big races.

Spa was next on the agenda and by this time I had decided, somewhat against the advice of the doctors, to have a plastic sleeve made up for my arm. I did not need to move the wrist much, but a plaster cast was too bulky in the narrow confines of a racing car, so I had the plaster taken off for Spa, and this plastic affair put on instead.

Everybody was a bit dubious about me driving, especially at Spa. Some of the press thought I had taken leave of my senses. 'Here's Stewart going to drive in this Belgian Grand Prix where he had his accident a couple of years ago and he's going to try and do it with one hand.' There was no strength in it at all, but it was only a case of being able to change gear with it and hold on to the steering wheel. With second fastest practice time I decided to start in the race although through not being very good at gearchanging, I made a poor getaway. It was difficult to snatch the gears without moving the wrist. I inherited the lead which had been held by Amon and Surtees and had a bit of a dice with

Denny which ended when his McLaren broke a drive shaft joint.

This put me half a minute ahead.

The car had been going perfectly, until on the left hander where Mike Parkes had his accident the year before, all of a sudden it gave a cough and a splutter. I thought if it were fuel starvation it would have something to do with surge, so I tried to ease it up the hill. It kept going, then cut out again, re-started, and then stopped completely. By the time I got to the hairpin there was just no fuel left and I knew that was the end of the line. I coasted into the pits, jumped out of the car and they put fuel in, jumped back in again and the car would not start. The battery was flat. I had started on my last lap and watched McLaren, Rodriguez (BRM) and Ickx (Ferrari) go past.

Fourth in Belgium was an appalling disappointment. But the press had been sympathetic, and this was an encouragement to Jackie. They had already almost given Graham the Championship but had been generous in their praise for Jackie's one-armed assault on the title. Graham failed to score at Spa because of a broken drive shaft and in fact failed to add to his total until the German Grand Prix much later. Yet Stewart in the Matra, although with a meagre three points after four races, was now in the fight.

After Spa I went back to Geneva. The doctor took off my plastic sleeve and put on a plaster cast again, giving me a dressing-down because I was in a lot of pain due to muscle exhaustion from the race. I could do no testing or Formula 2 racing at this time because of the need to conserve the arm for Grands Prix. We knew we were competitive and had to concentrate on Formula 1.

Zandvoort in Holland turned out to be a very tiring circuit for the arm because of all the bumps and undulations. The MS 10 did not take these lightly, there was a lot of kickback in the steering and it was hard work on the arms. I practised so much on the first day that the wrist swelled, and I could not drive the following afternoon. Chris Amon had fastest time in the Ferrari, Jochen was next with the Brabham, and Graham Hill was on the outside of the front row. Brabham was alongside me in the second row and in fact I was lucky not to get replaced there by Jacky Ickx in the Ferrari who was only 0.02 of a second behind me.

You get a feeling about luck, and at this point in time I felt it had deserted me. First there had been the accident at Jarama and the nagging doubt about whether or not the bone in my wrist was really damaged. Then the discovery that of all things to go wrong it had to be an irritating, tiny, hair-line crack that more or less had to break properly before it would ever mend. At Spa we felt we had run out of luck as well as petrol. But at Zandvoort it really took a turn for the better.

It rained.

I had done some wet weather testing with Dunlop but for this race, contrary to what everyone said afterwards, I did not have the new wet weather Dunlops on the car. Our weather forecast that morning was for intermittent rain. There was a good chance that the track would dry, and Dunlop feared in that event that the tyres would overheat and I might need to stop and change them. Jean-Pierre Beltoise used the new wet compound with a circumferential groove on the V12 Matra because he was going to have to stop for fuel in any case. But I set off with dry grooved Dunlops. There is no question that had it been dry I could not have completed the distance, never mind win. The arm became very painful indeed, but the slower pace was easy on it - you do not get the same sort of kick-back driving on a wet surface, wheel movements have to be smoother, and the steering is lighter.

Graham Hill led the race for three laps, but as the rain became heavier, Jackie narrowed the gap and overtook him. Thereafter he led for the remainder of the 90 laps on a track drenched with heavy showers throughout the afternoon. He lapped the entire field, until near the end Jean-Pierre Beltoise overtook him again to finish second, the only car on the same lap. Pedro Rodriguez (BRM) was third.

It was wet again for the French Grand Prix, and this time we made an error about the tyres. The ones we wanted to use did not have just the right qualities for Rouen.

All track surfaces round the world are slightly different. Certain tyres suit some tracks and not others. Conversely, there are tyres which do not register on one particular track. Rouen in the wet was just a circuit which did not suit the characteristics of the Dunlops we had on the car. It was not just me. Other Dunlop runners had similar trouble.

Jacky Ickx passed me in the Ferrari before the end of the first lap and then Jochen did the same, it was Firestone first and Goodyear second. I finished third behind Ickx and John Surtees in the Honda. I was not in business at all. I was not pleased with my personal performance, or the tyre performance, or even the car's performance. It was an unhappy occasion altogether and the race in which Jo Schlesser died.

Third at Rouen took Stewart to second equal place in the Championship. Jacky lckx and he had 16 points with one win, one third, and one fourth place apiece. Hill led with 24, Denny Hulme came after Stewart and lckx with 12 points and Pedro Rodriguez next with ten. Six races had gone, and there were six to go, the Grands Prix of Britain, Germany, Italy, Canada, the United States, and Mexico.

Next race was the British Grand Prix at Brands Hatch. I was still having my plastic cast removed and replaced twice a week. Here again we had a circuit which I knew was going to be hard work on the arm and in fact I had more pain in this race than in any other I have ever taken part in. Brands is exhausting enough when you are fit, with its bumps and adverse cambers and the Matra did not suit it. I thought of stopping many times, but I also knew that the World Championship was involved, there were points to be won and that was a colossal incentive. I drove with one hand for certainly half and probably two thirds of that race, I tried to catch John Surtees towards the end after his aerofoil had fallen off, but I failed by about half a length and finished sixth - all that effort for one point.

Jackie had to be lifted out of the car after that race, he was so completely drained. When he did get out, he was sick, and when they got him back to Geneva, he slept for eighteen hours. The doctors diagnosed severe exhaustion; he had used up his blood oxygen by driving himself so hard in his fight to keep racing despite the pain in his arm. Next night he slept for fourteen hours. His doctors despaired of the bone setting so long as he continued to race and were talking once again of a pinning operation. And the next race was Nürburgring.

I had decided to at least go to the Nürburgring and see what the prospects were. Ken was now getting enthusiastic about the Championship, he felt there was a chance. It was pouring with rain and even though we had only managed the third row of the grid I thought that I had better drive, or at least try. I put on my plastic sleeve again and helped, as at Zandvoort by the wet roads which eased the strain on the arm considerably, I did drive and suffered no ill effects whatever. The arm was sore, and once again I doubted if I would have been able to do two laps in the dry.

Throughout the race I had the story from Ken through pit signals. The conditions really were bad, in fact it was close to being an ill-advised race, the visibility in places was so poor. It was not so difficult for me being at the front because I only had my own spray to see through, but with the gloom of the fog and the spray from my own wheels it was difficult enough. I knew that in these conditions I had to get a lead and maintain it and increase it because you just never knew when you were going to get a bit sideways or lose time in a slide or something and you had to have a margin in hand if you could. Anyway, we won the race which brought thoughts of a World Championship a great deal closer, although Graham Hill finished second, which did not help at all.

For the first time we used an aerofoil. We had tried it in practice on the morning of the race, but we had been unable to do any testing with it. I felt it improved cornering, so we just left it on.

The German Grand Prix of 1968 was perhaps Jackie Stewart's greatest race ever. For three days the circuit high in the Eifel Mountains lay beneath the cloud-base. Practice was intermittent in the rain and fog. The road was wet in varying degrees throughout the period and the rain dripped incessantly on thousands of spectators camping in the woods. The shape of the starting grid was an unreliable guide to form, because a lot depended on when the time was put up and the prevailing conditions. Jacky Ickx was on pole with Amon and Rindt alongside him, then came

Hill and Elford who, like Ickx had an intimate knowledge of the course through touring car and rally-type events. On the third row, 50 seconds behind Ickx's practice time came Jackie Stewart. On a projection of this Ickx would have lapped Stewart well before the end of 14 laps.

Ickx made a poor start however, and by half-way round the first lap Stewart was in second place. Before the cars reached the end of the 28.29 km lap the blue Matra was in front by no less than 9 seconds. A lap later the lead was an almost incredible 34 seconds ahead of Hill. Then it reached 47 seconds, and then 58 seconds with only 9 seconds covering the next four cars, Hill, Amon, Rindt, and Ickx, followed by a gap of over a minute to Brabham and Hulme.

At twelve laps Stewart was two minutes in the lead. Rain still swept over the course, visibility in the darker parts of the circuit between the trees diminished further as the afternoon wore on. At the end Stewart crossed the line, brought the car back round the loop behind the pits, got out, sheltered from the rain, and chatted to officials before his pursuers could be even heard approaching. He had won by the astonishing margin of over four minutes, or nearly seven miles.

Even with second place at Nürburgring, Hill's lead in the World Championship was now reduced to four points. The next race, Monza could have been decisive.

We were in the leading bunch at Monza when the top end of the engine seemed to fall to pieces. This was disappointing because Graham had gone out after losing a wheel. He was becoming quite accomplished at driving on three wheels by this time of the year, but this one happened at a particularly difficult part of the course and there was not much he could do.

The scaphoid had enjoyed the unusually long gap between the Nürburgring and Monza and was now healing up. By Monza it was in fact nineteen weeks, so the surgeons had been about right, but their scepticism about how I was treating it was less justified. Dr Argand in Geneva was incredulous, he had practically given up hope of putting me right.

In Canada we qualified very poorly, row five of the grid to be exact. The car did not seem to have it in it, and maybe I was not going all that well either. The two of us were just not talking to each other. Early in the race for some unknown reason a wishbone broke, that is the top link on the front suspension which holds the wheel at the correct angle. It broke without any help from me, I had not hit anything. I came into the pits to retire and sat down on the barrier thinking maybe it's just as well- it was a beautiful day. When suddenly Ken rushed over and said, 'It's been fixed, we've mended it, get back into the car.' So, I had to put all my gear back on, face mask, helmet, and go back out again - it was like being caught knocking off work early in the afternoon.

It was a ninety lap race and I had lost several laps. Denny was leading at an easy pace, nobody was near him, and I began going round at a furious speed, making up two laps of my deficit from Denny and finishing sixth, picking up a solitary point which was a help, even though Graham collected three that day. He had been lucky, because the top engine mountings were pulling out of the monocoque, so really his car was threatening to break in two, so he had done very well to get fourth. Like me he was pursuing points avidly. With two races left he now had 33 and I had 27.

We had done some tyre testing prior to the United States Grand Prix and felt rather pessimistic, we felt we were not going to be quick enough. However, on the first day we actually posted fastest and second fastest times because I had taken out the spare car and was still faster than anyone else. Next day a hub carrier broke, and I went off the road luckily without damaging anything. Mario Andretti made the fastest time, which was a great feat. This was his first introduction to Grand Prix racing and to do it in front of an American crowd in a car that was not his own for the year was a great piece of driving. It endorsed the opinion I had gained of him at Indianapolis. He has great natural ability and is going to be an important figure in racing for a very long time.

We won the American Grand Prix with Graham second, so the scoring was still close, and there was now a clear chance of winning the Championship. Denny was in the hunt too after his great wins at Monza and Mosport. He had come up late in the season after earning just a few points earlier through consistency, 2 in South Africa, 6 in Spain, 2 in Monaco, 2 in France and 3 at Brands Hatch.

We all tripped back to London for the Earl's Court Motor Show and all the other things we had to do. There was nothing for it in the next few weeks but kick our heels and contemplate the possibility of winning or losing the World Championship. Graham Hill and I have basically a similar sense of humour and of course we took up postures in public and private to emphasise our rivalry.

It was very important for us to try and win, and it was important to Dunlop as well because they had lost at Le Mans. There had been every chance of them winning it in 1968 because they had already won the World Sports Car Championship with Porsche, but Ford snatched this important race away from them for Firestone. Dunlop were so keen for the World Championship that they flew £4,000s worth of tyres to Mexico to do some testing prior to the race. Unfortunately, the authorities changed their mind and would not allow us the testing session they had promised.

I did most of my tyre testing in practice and posted some fairly good times. I was out trying to improve them when a driveshaft broke, whipped up and hit the anti-roll bar, smashing this into a tyre which immediately blew up. This was on the main straight at about a hundred and fifty miles an hour. I went along trying to catch it and keep control, luckily managing, but by the time the car stopped the monocoque had been damaged. Ken managed to have it repaired for race day and I drove it although I had also qualified the spare car.

There was a lot of tension here because three people stood to win the World Championship. I certainly felt edgy and annoyed that, for example the night before the race I was involved in entertaining a whole lot of French journalists. I did not feel I should have to do this sort of thing at this time. Any other race would have been different, but the night before the outcome of the Championship ... I told Ken this on the way back from the hotel and very nearly fell out with him. He was optimistic, I was just the reverse and even this irritated me.

Attention at the track from the press and films and the public was very big. You really had to try and keep away from people and get some peace and quiet in the cool. I had tried to regulate my emotions to reduce the sense of occasion that I could not help experiencing. I had to try and face the race itself without feeling that the Championship was on my shoulders. It was essential to be cool in that broiling heat of Mexico City, and cool too in the heat of the battle for the title.

Graham was certainly in the strongest position mathematically. I felt we were competitive and Denny had an outside chance of winning, but he knew the only way he was going to do it was keep out of trouble and hope that both Graham and I would have problems. If I had won and Graham been second, I would still have won the Championship by virtue of more wins, even though the points total would have been equal. There were lots of permutations from which the possible winner was Hill but the only way I was going to win was finish well in front of him.

In the race Graham led for a bit, and then I led for a bit, and it really looked like being an epic race, especially when you considered that the Championship was being thrashed out in first and second places.

My car started to go off form early on. I noticed it was not pulling at the top of the engine speed range. This gradually became more noticeable as the race wore on, the speed at which it went 'flat' dropped and dropped until the engine was actually cutting out round corners. Finally, I lost six or seven seconds on one lap and Graham just disappeared into the distance.

I had to console myself with the fact that far from winning the Championship we might not finish at all, but we had to keep going. All sorts of things could still happen, and Denny had gone off the road after only 11 laps when his suspension broke. It was by no means impossible for Graham's car to fail - I don't mean I wanted his wheels to fall off again, just something to slow him.

The lap chart for this race is interesting if you trace my number 15 throughout. I occupied just about every position in the field from the lead to seventh where I finished, gaining places when cars dropped out, losing them again when I was overtaken next lap. My concern therefore was to finish so it was not over until the end as far as I was concerned although I think everyone else had given up.

Graham did not break down. He won the race fair and square which was a nice way to win the world title. Ken was terribly disappointed, more than I was really because I had had the chance to figure it all out while the race was still on.

In this respect the driver is luckier than the people in the pits because he knows precisely what is going on. It turned out to be a trifling enough fault. There is a pump on each side of the car feeding the petrol through to a central pick-up tank which leads to the engine. The gauze on the right-hand tank had broken up and some of the coating from inside had escaped up the connecting pipe. As soon as we went round a corner it blocked and gradually the silt got further and further into the system. The really important thing after not winning was to profit from the experience.

It was true we had demonstrated you could still get to Mexico with a chance, even though you had had a poor start to the season, but that is not when the overall contest is won. Most people in the first few races have new cars to settle in, or if they have not, they are still running interim models from the previous year. Graham had his championship won by the third event in the year, whereas we had not started to score until the fourth event.

As a result, we decided to start early for 1969 and this more than anything else was responsible for the 1969 success. We resolved to do all our testing in a heavy programme during January because the South African Grand Prix was going to be in March, and we had to be ready in good time. We were not going to start with old, used equipment. We had to have the engines and equipment to go ahead from a strong position from the first race to the last.

It had been a good year from my personal point of view even though I had suffered personal discomfort through my arm injury. I had certainly learned a lot through being again competitive in World Championship races - there is nothing like wins for restoring a driver's confidence. More important it gave the team confidence, in themselves, in me, and in the car. We also had the confidence of Dunlop and we had established ourselves amongst our rivals as a force to be reckoned with.

In a sense it was a good thing I did not win the title. Graham did the job superbly. If I had been Champion in 1968, I am not sure I would have been well prepared for it. They might have tabbed me boy wonder World Champion, but it would have been a lot for me to undertake and hope to do it as well as Graham.

The major lesson for me in the year was the self-control that I had learned and its effect on my race performances. I had learned to start a race cleanly without emotional interference in my driving. This had been necessary partly because of the big sporting occasion that a Grand Prix is. A driver has an enormous responsibility to his team, the manufacturers of his car, his tyre and components as well as himself and the people who have paid to watch the race either at the circuit or on television. This is an awesome thought, a very daunting one.

I had started to learn the principle in 1968 although it showed itself more in 1969. It was something that I had to develop late in the season, in particular at Nürburgring and Watkins Glen and Mexico. Then I realised that this was something I had to cultivate deliberately. At first, I just could not explain it and then it dawned on me that something was there and there was a reason for it.

It is nothing to do with natural ability whatever that is. It is something that you first experience and then exploit. It was something Jim Clark did not always have although he certainly brought it into play later in his career. I found out that in the right frame of mind I could go out and hit a good lap time almost immediately through being in complete control of myself, through having arranged a mental build-up starting the day before.

First, I must not get myself into an optimistic mood. I must not be particularly jovial or be with parties or noisy groups of people. I like to be with people with whom I do not have to 'try', that is to say people with whom I do not have to make conversation, people I can relax with. The journalists I had to help entertain that night before the Mexican Grand Prix was a case in point. I liked them, they were interested in me, talking to them is an essential part of my business, but not that night. It interrupted the CountDown. It starts when I go to bed. I have to get into neutral and fall asleep naturally, not by counting sheep or anything like that. I tend to wake up earlier, but this is becoming less critical. It used to be 6 am and then 6.30 and then 7, which was all a part of playing down the occasion. Then, instead of lying awake thinking about the race or the weather or who has been quicker than me in practice I want a good book, or something to hold my interest. I realise it is an important day; I realise that I have a Grand Prix to do, and I can become rather tense.

The closest analogy is that I am like a bouncy sort of ball and towards the time of the race I have to progressively deflate. All the air has to be let out by a deliberate mental process. If the ball remains too hard it has too much bounce and it is difficult to control, but if it is flat and unemotional it will do nothing unexpected.

I sometimes read myself to sleep again and when I wake, I will not want breakfast. I like to start a race a little bit hungry just to sharpen my wits. By the time I walk to the pits the ball is going down, consciously deflating, getting tired and heavy. By this time, I have blunted the nervousness and by the time it comes to sit in the car I have for all practical purposes no emotion left, it has been drained away. Everyone else can be getting tweaked up, the mechanics, Ken, Helen even, yet when the five-minute signal goes, I can really feel, 'What a waste of time all this is, I should not be in the car, I should be out in the cooler air.' Being so detached helps you to think clearly, there must be no confusion at this stage. I want the mechanics close, in case the engine fails to start and I can make sure about the last few items on the mental checklist calmly.

When the flag falls there is no emotion left at all. I see the man with the flag, and then the flag going up and falling just like you would when waiting at traffic lights in a familiar street and with no more excitement. I can thus try to make a deliberate start and go for the first comer, set the car up for the apex with no more excitement or drama than I would if it were the fiftieth lap of the race.

What Jackie Stewart aims at in exercising this control is to try and set the pace of a race in the opening laps, to try and take command of the race as early as he can. It is interesting to see in a film that Austin Campbell made of him in 1969 that he achieves this at Monaco, a circuit where the first few laps are especially critical. Campbell's cameramen followed him from his hotel room right to the starting grid and you can almost see the ball going down. He walks down the hill to the start acknowledging the acclaim of spectators, signing autographs, and utterly unperturbed by the great sporting occasion that the Monaco Grand Prix is, and that he knows it is. When he kisses Helen before he goes to the car it is entirely dispassionate even though it is quite clear that she is afraid. He has quite thought himself into a sort of personality change. The film shows him to be completely physically relaxed apart from his eyes which are very intense. In fact, he uses his eyes to shoo away autograph hunters. His count-down is almost complete and there is no room for extraneous activities. He will chat to friends or journalists or people he has something to say to. He is not, unlike some of the other drivers with whom he will share the grid, aggressive, or extra talkative or morose and it is a mark of how he matured during that critical 1968 season that he has attained this control by a very, very intelligent approach to the subject.

His rivals are rarely as self-sufficient during the opening laps of a Grand Prix. This is why drivers like Jo Siffert sometimes glance off the kerb in the first few laps. Jochen Rindt probably comes closest to Jackie in controlling first lap nerves but even he makes little mistakes. Jacky Ickx takes a lap or two to get the hang of things and has made some notably poor starts like at the Nurburgring in 1968 when it was so essential to get clear of other cars' spray and he had pole position. Denny Hulme rarely snatches an early lead in a race because he seems to know he takes a few laps to adjust, and he drives accordingly. Stewart claims that he can often tell what a driver is going to do in the first few laps of a race by his personality, and conversely his personality shows through by how he behaves in the opening stages of a race. Graham Hill does not go barging into things in the opening laps, he takes it cautiously at first because he knows that he is not yet ready to go all out. Similarly, Hill in practice takes several laps to get down to his time and he does not like to go quickly until he feels his car is just right.

Stewart was now on the threshold of his Championship Year. Mentally better equipped than at any time since he began racing to put up a challenging performance, he had finally lost the 'Boy Wonder' label. He was now accepted as one of the Grand Prix 'regulars'. Since he arrived on the scene in 1965 there had been many changes, and while he does not aspire to the status of 'veteran' like Brabham or Hill, four years is quite a long time in Grand Prix racing.

Yet a World Championship, even in the fifth year of Grand Prix racing, is a rare achievement. Some Grand Prix drivers never win a Grand Prix throughout their career. Only ten men had won the World Championship since it was instituted in 1950. Giuseppe Farina (1950), Juan Manuel Fangio (1951, 1954, 1955, 1956, 1957), Alberto Ascari (1952, 1953), Mike Hawthorn (1958), Graham Hill (1962, 1968), Jim Clark (1963, 1965), John Surtees (1964), and Denny Hulme (1967).

In 1969 Jackie Stewart made it eleven.

The MS 80 Matra, Monte Carlo 1969.

The Formula 2 Matra in an Easter race at Thruxton.

PART TWO

The 1969 season

5.

Kyalami, the South African Grand Prix

South Africa, March 1st, 1969, Kyalami circuit, 2.55 miles to the lap, race distance 80 laps 204 miles. The track lies close by the main Johannesburg-Pretoria road about 20 miles from the centre of Johannesburg. There were 18 starters in the race and 9 finishers. The lap record stood to Jim Clark who won the 1968 race, at 1 min 23.7 sec., a speed of 109.68 mph. The starting grid in 1969 was as follows:

Brabham (Brabhams-Ford) 1.20.0		**Rindt** (Lotus-Ford) 1.20.2		**Hulme** (McLaren-Ford) 1.20.3
	Stewart (Matra-Ford) 1.20.4		**Amon** (Ferrari) 1.20.5	
Andretti (Lotus-Ford) 1.20.8		**Hill** (Lotus-Ford) 1.21.1		**McLaren** (McLaren-Ford) 1.21.1
	van Rooyen (Mclaren-Ford) 1.21.8		**Love** (Lotus-Ford) 1.22.1	
Beltoise (Matra-Ford) 1.22.2		**Siffert** (Lotus-Ford) 1.22.2		**Ickx** (Brabham-Ford) 1.23.1
	Oliver (BRM) 1.24.1		**Rodriguez** (BRM) 1.25.2	
de Klerk (Reco-Brabham) 1.27.1		**Tingle** (Reco-Brabham) 1.50.4		**Surtees** (BRM) *no official time owing to a technicality*

The result was :

1st Jackie Stewart (Matra-Ford), 1 hour 50 mins. 39.1 sec. 110.62 mph.

2nd Graham Hill (Lotus-Ford), 1 hour 50 mins. 57.9 sec. 110.31 mph.

3rd Denny Hulme (McLaren-Ford), 1 hour 51 mins. 10.9 sec. 110,09 mph.

4th Jo Siffert (Lotus-Ford), 1 hour 51 mins. 28.3 sec. 109.80 mph.

5th Bruce McLaren (McLaren-Ford) 79 laps.

6th Jean-Pierre Beltoise (Matra-Ford) 78 laps.

7th Jackie Oliver (BRM) 77 laps.

8th Sam Tingle (Repco-Brabham) 73 laps.

Fastest lap, Stewart, lap 50, 1 min. 21.6 sec. 112.5 mph. Running at the end of the race but not classified as a finisher; Peter de Klerk (Repco-Brabham).

Championship points: Stewart 9 points. Hill 6 points. Hulme 4 points. Siffert 3 points. McLaren 2 points. Beltoise 1 point.

Kyalami is one of the most enjoyable events on the calendar for several reasons, not the least of which is the glorious weather. The race this year was in March instead of January when it used to coincide with Hogmanay. The hottest period of the summer had in theory gone although when we were tyre testing in late February it was the hottest they had had for forty years.

I had gone to South Africa on 22nd February, very comfortably by Alitalia because I had flown from Geneva to Rome. Arrival at Johannesburg is an unpleasant business. You are kept in the aircraft while an official sprays the interior from an aerosol can as though you all had foot-and mouth. Your baggage takes a long time to be hauled by a porter almost certainly being shouted at. All the airport staff seem to be tall and wear short trousers, looking slightly absurd to begin with until you see the sense of it in that climate.

Flying to South Africa is perhaps the most trying of the year's trips. Generally, I sleep fairly well in a jet, but I get dehydrated and welcome the sanctuary of the

Kyalami Ranch which is almost within walking distance of the circuit. I have to drink quite a lot of fluids on the journey to remain moist so when I reach the Ranch, usually just before lunchtime, having been flying all night, I enjoy a shower and then a light meal in the air-conditioned dining room. A real refuge for a tired traveller. They also have a beautiful swimming pool around which most of the rooms or chalets are grouped. The only trouble with the Kyalami Ranch is that the service is so bad. I value service more than almost anything else in an hotel and it really is poor here. They have a serious staff problem and so you have to be very tolerant.

I try to remain awake the day I arrive so by the evening I'm pretty washed out and get to bed early. Ken Tyrrell and Dunlop expect their driver to rise early for tyre testing somewhere about seven next morning. It is not too difficult, because by then you have shaken off jet fatigue.

The early start and the heat and the physically demanding work of tyre testing mean that I try to have either completed the morning's tests or else show enough eagerness to stop by 11.30 or 12 noon that Ken and Iain Mills and Alec Meskell of Dunlop have taken notice. At the first chance I get out of the Matra and into my Ford from the Ranch and get back to the air conditioning or the swimming pool. I find it essential to have around an hour and a half or two hours off at lunchtime. Try and keep this in mind, Ken.

Kyalami is one of the world's best circuits for car and tyre analysis. It is undulating, well-surfaced, and wellkept. It is a suitable circuit for analysis because it includes some critically shaped corners with enough straight between them for the driver to figure out how the car is behaving.

There is one double apex corner, that is to say two corners which you take as one, and then the road goes 'off camber', slopes away from the inside instead of being banked naturally. You go downhill on a very rough, corrugated part of the circuit which was unfortunately not bottomed deeply enough when it was built. They have re-surfaced it but the suspension is still really tortured here. Yet the sequence will tell you a great deal about the car and the tyres, and how they are behaving in relation to one another.

The Esses is another significant place. It is a left-hand corner followed quickly by a right hander, which you take in third gear. It is difficult because you cannot take the left hander too quickly or the car will not react to the change of direction between the bends. It is good for analysing because it shows up the need for a responsive car that does not heel over or slide too much.

Much the best thing about South Africa is the annual encounter with Alex Blignaut. He is the man in charge there in every possible way. The organisers have a very difficult race to run. They have to bring everyone out from Europe, which is an expensive business and yet they have one of the best-run races in the world. Much of what they have achieved they owe to Alex.

He tends to be very aggressive at first; he wants to give you the impression he doesn't care a damn for you when he first meets you. 'So,' he will say, 'you've come back have you, well you're not going to get any more money out of me.' You nearly back out of his office door because all this is likely to come at you in a torrent. 'Take things as they are or you're not going to have them at all. So, you want a safety barrier up here, who do you think you are? I don't think a safety barrier's any good anyway. Nobody's ever been killed there in any case.' So, you have to shout back at him, 'Look, for God's sake, Alex, I'm not putting up with this, we get this every year from you. Now behave yourself and let's talk business.'

After about a quarter of an hour Blignaut settles down and he has decided that he is not going to be aggressive to you any more, and really you are not going to cause him any inconvenience. By the end of the day, he will have you out at the track asking what other barriers you would like to put up, because he wants to have the best track in the world, and the safest track in the world. And if money earned from motor racing can buy it, he will have it. Alex is one of the best and most co-operative organisers that we have.

When we are tyre testing he charges only for the special facilities that we ask for, such as the doctor, ambulance, fire-fighters and security men we have as marshals on every comer. Blignaut sets all this up very efficiently even though every year we go through the same fighting routine, and I am sure he enjoys it all as much as I do, it is part of the experience of going to Kyalami.

Another thing you have to take into account is the height of about 5,000 feet above sea level. This makes a big difference because there is less oxygen in the air. We lose almost 20 per cent of the engine's power and this makes a dent in the car's performance. It is the same for everyone of course, but it does affect each car and it is immediately noticeable. It made the Matra feel like a Formula 2 car. You feel it particularly in acceleration and you can tum the power on without worrying too much about wheelspin.

You get the same thing in Mexico City, which is even higher, so much that it affects people as well. I can get out of breath there if I am doing anything strenuous although I have never experienced that in South Africa.

Kyalami is certainly not the world's most difficult course. There are quite a lot of places where you can overtake. You can do it at the end of the straight, or going into the first left hander of the Esses if you are a little bit cheeky. Or you can outbrake somebody going into Clubhouse if he co-operates but you have trouble if he does not. There are no particularly alarming or frightening features, it is straightforward unless it rains and then it becomes especially treacherous.

With the rain you get in South Africa, the circuit becomes completely flooded. All the drains become choked, there are rivers crossing it and very deep puddles. Kyalami in the rain is something else altogether. I have only driven there in the wet a couple of times. Even the locals do not know where the puddles will be, because the track changes every lap as banks break or ditches fill up.

There are still facilities required at Kyalami. It is a bit primitive in some respects, for example if you want something to eat. But it is being built up and it is one of the few circuits in the world where they are prepared to spend money, and even admit they are making money. Their costs are perhaps higher than any comparable European Grand Prix. Yet they can still make money out of it by good promotion locally. You cannot help being disappointed by those characters in European motor racing who do not seem able - or refuse to admit that they are able - to afford the things that are required.

One takes a few special precautions in South Africa to combat the heat. Cockpit cooling is very important, and you have to ensure that the driver's space is completely blocked off from hot air streams that could reach you from the radiator, or the oil coolers. The cockpit must be properly ventilated with fresh, cool air from outside. Pedal apertures are a source of trouble, and they have to be sealed off with tape and sponge and so forth, because they could give a lot of difficulties in a race. I have had feet blistered in a racing car and that can distract and slow you.

Except for maintaining the usual standard of fitness there is very little that I do personally to combat the climate. I find that I cannot drink too much because I can get a curious kind of tummy cramp from drinking cold things in hot weather. I take tablets to replace the salt lost in perspiration although I am not absolutely sure I need them because I have never gone without them.

I have made a lot of friends in the years since I first raced in South Africa. Basil van Rooyen for example whom I met when I came over for that first Rand Grand Prix. He is a very talented driver, one of the best in South Africa. The Rand Grand Prix in 1964 also featured a saloon car race in which I drove a Lotus Cortina for Team Lotus in place of Jimmy Clark.

Basil, I think was very upset that Jimmy was not driving and this unknown Scotsman had come to take his place because here, he felt was his big opportunity to show South Africa and perhaps the world that he was going to beat Jim Clark in a Lotus Cortina. As it happened, I was rather afraid he might, because Basil had made the horsepower and performance of his car sound very intimidating. I felt it would be terrible to drive a Group 2 Lotus Cortina for the factory and be beaten. As it happened, I was quicker in practice and finished second in the race only to Paul Hawkins's Galaxie, winning the class and beating Basil who was fourth I think behind another Galaxie or a Falcon.

John Love is a Rhodesian, and he is pretty close to us in South Africa because he was one of Ken's 'discoveries'. He drove for Ken in Formula Junior; they are about the same age, and they certainly get on well together. John is a very quiet individual, but he is as hard as nails. I first met him one blustery day at Silverstone in 1964. He was over on vacation and John Cooper had talked him into driving a Mini in some race or other, and we all went to Silverstone for the day, because we also had Formula 3 cars to test. Love did not have a very good day. He got all crossed up and went off at Chapel for some reason which was quite difficult to do in a Formula 3 car. He spun and damaged the car.

Not satisfied with that he stuffed a Mini Cooper straight into the bank at Woodcote, overturning and completely destroying it. All of which was disappointing to everyone because it was just prior to the Gold Cup at Oulton and he was going to drive a works Mini in one race and the Formula 3 in another.

It was not a good time for Ken either. When we got to Oulton Park, I turned my Formula 3 Cooper end over end at Lodge. Love is still a big hero in South Africa, and a great character. He prepares his cars very well and races them well yet does not seem to want to come back to drive again in Europe although he has had many opportunities.

The South African Grand Prix was the first race of the new season. Drivers were shaking down with their new teams, and some cars were barely completed in the weeks or even days immediately before the race. Jochen Rindt had just joined Gold Leaf Team Lotus, replacing Jackie Oliver who had gone to BRM. lckx was with Brabham, having left Ferrari. Surtees led the BRM team which had a new version of the V12 engine with four valves per cylinder only run for the first time a week before first practice. Ferrari had a new version of its V12 and Brabham had finally discarded the faithful Repco V8, after two World Championships and which had finally over-reached itself. The FordCosworth, exclusive to Lotus in 1967, used additionally by Matra and McLaren in 1968, was now also in the Brabhams. It was also reaching private teams. Making one of his rare appearances with Lotus was American driver Mario Andretti who had been so promising in the US Grand Prix the previous year, and Jean-Pierre Beltoise joined Jackie Stewart in Matra International as a temporary measure, 'until the Matra V12 is ready'.

Aerofoils were now in general use. They had become regular wear towards the end of 1968 even though always subject to debate. Their purpose was to produce a downforce by air acting on the *wing the opposite way to an aircraft's, namely downwards. This pressed the tyres down into the road, increasing their grip. Some people were apprehensive, lest for example the car spun and went backwards; it would then have lift instead of downforce and the whole thing might take off. Some wings had broken loose during races and one at least had lofted at speed into the grandstand at Brands Hatch. Fortunately, it happened during a private test session and there was no one in the grandstand at the time. The Great Wing Accident was still to come, but Kyalami lent credence to their critics.*

There were some tense moments in the Lotus pit during practice at Kyalami. Mario Andretti was billed very highly. The South Africans wanted something to talk about, and this was Mario, the first American Grand Prix driver since Dan Gurney and an Italian American which was even better. Here he was in the Lotus camp and Mario is very quick, Jochen and Graham were pretty concerned about who was going to have the best car and the best engine. I must confess the rest of us were being a bit mischievous, giving Jochen a 'tip-off' that Graham was hiding a spare V8 in his hotel room, or telling Graham that Jochen had some special bits and pieces on his car and was passing everybody down the straight. Mario on the other hand seemed to prefer lying by the pool, trusting Colin Chapman's sense of fair play. The other two did not seem to share his confidence. It was all very amusing.

As it happened, Jochen was quickest of the three, then Mario, and then Graham. Jochen has very set ideas. He seemed to make up his mind he was going to be fastest and when Jochen makes up his mind about something he goes straight for it. That was how he felt about that practice time. He was second fastest overall and took the middle of the front row of the grid.

I had seen something of the Surtees relationship with BRM during private practice and I really feared that it was not going to work out. It did not look as though the team was fitting together very well. They did not appear to have the power they had hoped for from the new engine and it was a V12. Events had by this time shown that a V8 was the racing engine to have.

Jacky lckx on the other hand was now driving a Ford Cosworth V8 and his performances in the past had given us all reason to think that in a Brabham, (with which the driver has a lot of freedom), he would be very fast against some of the more precise machines like the Lotus. Oddly, he never showed his potential in this race and it was left to Jack who went very, very fast and took pole position. This was unexpected and Jacky was a bit despondent but Brabham was really showing great form. The McLarens were doing well also. Denny had been out doing some testing at Kyalami and he was in the third car making up the front row.

We had the new Matra in South Africa, the MS 80. This had only just been completed and tested by Jean-Pierre briefly to see if there was any oil or water leaks before coming to South Africa. We used it in practice but decided against using it in the race. The MS 10 was still competitive, and the new one kept having engine trouble. It was thought to be an electrical problem, and then fuel trouble; no one seemed to have an answer so rather than spend time working on it we thought it would be better to remain with the older car.

The Ferrari achieved a good practice time. It was as quick as I was but never did many laps at a time, which made us suspect it had overheating trouble. You are always trying to discover rivals' weaknesses during practice and conceal your own. In this case we were right, the car did have overheating trouble and did not quite achieve half the race distance.

The starting grid is curious at Kyalami because pole position is on the outside or left side of the road which seems to be quite wrong for the first comer. Hulme was on the inside which really should be pole in my opinion. Ideally, the line for the first corner starts on the left side of the road, but in practice you can almost always dive up the inside on the first lap and the advantage goes to the car on the right of the road.

I was in row two on the left with Jochen Rindt's rear tyre just ahead on my right, and Brabham's rear in front and to the left. There was insufficient space to hope of getting between them when the flag went down. But I got a tremendous start. Everything just worked together, I had not too much wheelspin when I let in the clutch, the revs were just right and with a little S-shaped manoeuvre I went between the cars in front and by the time we reached the first comer I was in the lead.

That was the story of the entire South African Grand Prix. Stewart never relinquished the lead he gained at the start. He built it up in the opening laps and thereafter was able to set his own pace, taking full control of the race without over-stressing the car or himself for the full 80 laps. There was a shower of rain during practice, but the cloudy threat on race day never materialised.

Mario had a bad start and I knew I would have to keep my eye on him. Jack Brabham was behind until he went out with wing trouble and then there was Graham, but Ken kept me well informed of the gap. Just as Mario threatened to come up from behind Graham somebody had leaked a lot of oil round the circuit and Mario seemed to be getting a better grip with his Firestones than I had with the Dunlops. My tyres were never very good on an oily surface and I had to hold my pace until the oil cleared. But by then Mario had retired with transmission trouble so the threat to Graham's second place (and also to me because Mario would have tried very hard to catch up) went with him down the pit road.

As the race wore on, I could afford to smooth my driving out to make the car last. Instead of taking the engine to 10,000 rpm or whatever the limit would be, I started using 9,500 or a little less sometimes. Braking could be gentler and a little earlier so that cornering was less vicious. Smoothness paid off because the smoother your driving becomes, very often the faster you go. You employ more care in driving at a pace you set yourself to conserve the car and this is a nice position to be in because once you reach this level it is easier to improve on it. At Kyalami I had to put in a fast one half-way through the race, I had a clear track on lap and took the opportunity of 'turning up the wick' a little and gaining the lap record.

There was great glee in the greetings after the race from Ken and the Dunlop team. We go out to win every race, but this was one for which we had made a very special effort. We had gone out to South Africa early, prepared well, told Matra we meant to start the season successfully to consolidate our position as early in the year as we could and here we had done it. It is not often you get everything going for you the way it did for us at Kyalami. It is not even that you always feel that you have deserved to win a motor race, but this was one that the entire team deserved. It was a great boost to their confidence very fittingly because they had worked hard for it. The mechanics had been working sometimes from five in the morning to eight at night under very difficult, hot conditions.

We had champagne to celebrate and waited for the crowd to leave, which took much too long. This is one of the disadvantages of Kyalami, there is complete chaos when the race ends and all the spectators climb into their cars and they all try to get out of the gate together.

I eventually went back to the Kyalami Ranch as darkness fell, had a swim and a shower and a meal which Dunlop gave for the team and a few journalists. I am often more tired than I was after this race, despite the warm weather and went to a party at Paddy Driver's. I was so elated at having won the very first race of the season but unfortunately Paddy's party had almost ended by the time we got there. The evening had brought torrential rain and we splashed our way through the sandy scrub country to Paddy's farmhouse and started it going again. Paddy's hospitality over the years has been wonderful, as has that of another great friend in South Africa, Danny Alderton. They are both great enthusiasts, and people whose company I enjoy enormously. The South African Motor Racing Club have a relaxing prizegiving at their President Francis Tucker's home in one of the beautiful suburbs of Johannesburg. It is held in the gardens and really is a wonderful open-air party in the sunshine. The drivers love this sort of thing, which compares well with the more decorous, staid affairs you can find elsewhere.

And it's so good to take some money off Alex Blignaut at the end of the week.

6.

Barcelona, the Spanish Grand Prix

Barcelona, Spain, 4th May, 1969. 2.36 miles to the lap, race distance, 90 laps, 210 miles. The Montjuich Park Circuit is a dramatic, hillside track close to the centre of Barcelona. It is very twisty with no real straight and some very sharp corners. There were 14 starters in 1969 and only five cars finished. The previous lap record of 1 min. 38.3 sec., at 90.88 mph was set up by Jochen Rindt (Brabham-Ford) in a Formula 2 race because this Spanish Grand Prix was the first Formula 1 race ever held here. The starting grid was as follows:

Rindt (Lotus-Ford) 1.25.7		**Amon** (Ferrari) 1.26.2		**Hill** (Lotus-Ford) 1.26.6
	Stewart (Matra-Ford) 1.26.9		**Brabham** (Brabham-Ford) 1.27.8	
Siffert (Lotus-Ford) 1.28.2		**Ickx** (Brabham-Ford) 1.28.4		**Hulme** (McLaren-Ford) 1.28.8
	Surtees (BRM) 1.28.9		**Oliver** (BRM) 1.29.7	
Courage (Brabham-Ford) 1.29.3		**Beltoise** (Matra-Ford) 1.29.5		**McLaren** (McLaren-Ford) 1.29.71
	Rodriguez (BRM) 1.34.1			

The result was:

1st Jackie Stewart (Matra-Ford) 2 hours 16 mins. 53.0 sec. 93.45mph

2nd Bruce McLaren (McLaren-Ford) 88 laps.

3rd Jean-Pierre Beltoise (Matra-Ford) 87 laps

4th Denny Hulme (McLaren-Ford) 87 laps.

5th John Surtees (BRM) 84 laps.

6th Jacky Ickx (Brabham-Ford) 83 laps.

Fastest lap, Jochen Rindt (Lotus-Ford) 1.28.3, 96.59 mph.

World Championship points after Barcelona: 1st Stewart 18 points. 2nd McLaren 8 points. 3rd Hulme 7 points. 4th Hill 6 points. 5th Beltoise 5 points. 6th Siffert 3 points. 7th Surtees 2 points. 8th Ickx 1 point.

The organisers had made a wonderful job of getting this real road circuit as safe as they could. It was difficult and had cost them a lot of money. They had lined it entirely with Armco barriers at the behest of the drivers and the CSI, especially Ing. Bacciagaluppi. Jochen had checked it out beforehand and said he was satisfied with it, which as events turned out was just as well. Barcelona is unusual with many different sorts of corners. Much of it had been re-surfaced and it is a tiring circuit where drivers have to work very hard. I had a lot of engine trouble in practice getting gear ratios to suit all the different gradients and corners.

Racing engines work best at certain speeds. During practice therefore, drivers choose gear ratios which best suit the characteristics of their engine on different parts of the course. This is done largely by trial and error and involves substitution of different sized gearwheels in the gearbox, or perhaps changing the crown wheel and pinion.

Barcelona is what I call a graunchy circuit. It does not need driving ability so much as concentration and hard work, rather like Monte Carlo. This was the MS 80 Matra's second race. It never went well throughout practice and I made fourth fastest time nearly a second slower than Jochen who was on pole position.

There was a major drama at the start when Jackie Oliver's BRM burst an oil pipe and laid a carpet of oil all round the track on the warming-up lap. The officials were very co operative and allowed another exploratory lap so that we could find where all the oil was, but the police were just the opposite. Police on

Jackie Stewart on one of the fast bends of the Clermont-Ferrand circuit.

The Spanish Grand Prix; the last Formula 1 race with unrestricted aerofoil wings.

Jacky Ickx's wing failure in the Spanish Grand Prix.

Four-wheel drive Matra, the MS 84. First appearance at Zandvoort Dutch Grand Prix.

occasions like this can be quite impossible. They get very excited, they know nothing about motor racing and on this occasion really got up people's backs. In fact, they were partly to blame for the whole affair because they had shooed the BRM mechanics off the grid who were trying to get Jackie Oliver to stop the engine. Then, when the field did finally get off Piers Courage's car stalled on the line and the police would not let his mechanics on to the track to either start the engine or even push him away.

Jackie inherited the lead rather than won the Spanish Grand Prix. On lap one he was a lowly sixth after one of the poorest starts he made throughout the season. Ahead of him were Rindt, Amon, Siffert, Hill, and Brabham in that order. Hill and Rindt crashed heavily at the same part of the course within a few laps of one another for the same reason. Their aerofoil wings broke. The Lotus wings were keeping the cars' wheels on the ground, over a crest on the fastest part of the course, the 140 mph straight past the pits. Following the crest was a short downhill stretch where drivers had to brake hard and steer into a sharp, left-handed hairpin bend. It was a place where they needed all the wheel grip they could get.

First Hill, when the race was barely eight laps old came over the crest, trailing his wing behind. Deprived of its downthrust, the car took off and smashed itself against the barriers beside the road. A few laps later, Rindt who was in the lead did almost precisely the same, colliding with the wreckage of Hill's car and overturning. Hill was almost unhurt, but Rindt had head and face injuries.

Amon took the lead until the Ferrari's engine ran its bearings, Siffert went out when he broke an oil pipe and almost destroyed his engine. Brabham and he were the only cars Jackie actually overtook. Afterwards Ken Tyrrell said it was the one race the team would have won even if he (Tyrrell) had been driving.

I felt as though I had stolen this race. It is certainly the win of which I am the least proud. My car was not quite leaving the ground at this crest but even with our lower aerofoils I was getting wheelspin in top gear at around 140 mph. Just as I approached it on my eighth lap there were yellow flags being waved vigorously everywhere. You always get some indication of what sort of an obstruction it is by how the flag marshals behave, and the way they were waving this time I realised that something fairly big had happened just over the hill.

First thing was to brake and slow and when I had reached the brow and gone down a few gears I found wreckage all over the road. The first thought was to find out who has been involved. You could see the skid marks going to the left and then Graham's car lying over on the right with Graham getting out of it. It was an enormous relief to see that he was all right. Then I had to turn my attention back to what I was doing, which was picking a way through the debris because it is all too easy to collect a puncture after an accident, or worse get something lodged in the car somewhere.

Each time you come round you must decide what speed is safe through the accident area. I had just caught up on Jo Siffert, but he widened the gap under the yellow flag because he felt he could steer through the bits and pieces lying around the road faster than I did.

I tried to signal to the Lotus pit that Graham was on his feet. For the next few laps, I could see him examining the car obviously trying to make out what had broken. It was fairly clear even to me that something had broken. He then went down on his hands and knees beside the car.

A few laps later, there were the yellow flags once again. Jochen had had his accident in the same place. I could see him in the cockpit when I went past. He was still in the car, but they were trying to get him out and he was moving. Although his face was covered in blood he was moving in an active sort of way and I knew he was all right. By 'all right' I mean that the accident had not been a catastrophe. He was 'all right' in my book.

The terrible thing was that I had seen Graham underneath his car and Jochen had collided with it very hard indeed. Next lap my worst fears were, it seemed, confirmed. A marshal on the accident side of the road was talking to someone opposite. I saw rather than heard the conversation. There were a lot of people milling around but what I saw this man doing struck a bolt of horror into me. He drew his finger across his throat.

I was straightaway very frightened for Graham. I had not seen him again and it seemed certain that Jochen's car had hit Graham's with Graham still underneath. The marshal's sign was unmistakable and for the rest of the race I drove round convinced that Graham Hill had been killed.

It is a terrifying moment for a racing driver when he passes such an accident. We do not discuss things like this amongst ourselves very much, but I feel that most Grand Prix drivers react in much the same way. I isolate myself immediately. I lock myself into a numb condition, without any feeling or emotion until after the race. One has to do that. I knew it was a very big accident, but I did not feel physically sick or ill or anything like that, just numb. I am shocked afterwards that I could be capable of shutting the thing off till the race is finished. I even think, 'You really are a hard case. You should feel something when this happens.' But it is not like that at all. In some ways I am much too emotional but it is a part of my life that I have forced upon myself.

It was the same with Jo Schlesser's terrible accident at Rouen in 1968. There again I knew it was a dreadful accident, I did not see how anyone could have got out of that car, and of course poor Jo did not. I did not know whose car it was I could not recognise the broken wheels lying around or see what make it was through the smoke and flames. I kept looking in my mirror, seeing who was behind me, recognising friends who were still running and saying to myself, 'Well it's not him - so-and-so's all right.'

The sadness of losing a friend in a motor race can desolate you. But only after the motor race.

At Rouen I came into the pits to change tyres shortly after the accident and someone told me about Jo. Ken nearly threw him out of the pit. I have never seen Ken so wild. He knows how news like that could upset anyone still on the track, facing the same sort of dangers that had just claimed Schlesser.

At Barcelona Stewart, disturbed by the twin accident but still driving fast round Montjuich Park began to catch Chris Amon's failing Ferrari. He cut down the lead by about seven seconds during the final ten laps of Amon's drive but before he came to grips with the New Zealander his Ferrari engine expired in a cloud of blue smoke.

With a huge sense of relief hearing that my ideas of Graham's demise were exaggerated, I had afterwards to do some organising for Jochen's wife, Nina. She had been rather deserted by the Lotus team who had not appreciated how bad Jochen's injuries were. They thought he would get out of hospital the next day, that he had had nothing worse than a shaking.

The wife of a racing driver can have a very difficult time following an accident. She can be in a shocked condition herself and at this time Nina Rindt needed someone who could take charge of things. Jochen wanted to be taken home and I began to arrange with Executive Jet Services of Basle for a Lear Jet. Then I spoke to the surgeon Dr Soler Roig, father of Alex Soler Roig the Spanish racing driver. He told me that Jochen had a fractured upper jaw and a night's sleep was necessary for them to assess any other damage such as concussion.

Helen remained in Barcelona with Nina for a few days and eventually we got Jochen home and under repair. Once again there were safety lessons to be learned from the accident. It taught us how important it was on a circuit like Montjuich, which is almost totally enclosed by barriers to have facilities for removing wrecked cars from the track. Neither Lotus was a runner and there was no practical way of getting them out of people's way until a section of the barrier could be removed. This took time.

The presence of the barriers bordering the whole circuit meant that your driving had to be very accurate. There was no room for mistakes, and no latitude on corners. But there is no doubt in my mind that the Spanish organisers saved the lives of Graham Hill and Jochen Rindt. Not only that, but they also saved the lives of many spectators. As it was there were injuries, one man lost an eye and another had a broken arm through flying debris, but it could have been very, very much worse.

Two more important lessons emerged from Barcelona. First, the barriers were at a place where you would not normally expect an accident to happen. There are lots of circuits where the GPDA asks for a barrier and are met with an incredulous, 'We've never had an accident there. You won't need a barrier.' At Barcelona they took our word that the whole track needed barriers and let there be no mistake, they prevented what would certainly have been a tragedy of 1955 Le Mans proportions.

Furthermore, Barcelona will continue to have Grand Prix and Formula 2 races on the Montjuich circuit. But for the safety barriers, deaths and injuries would have been on such a scale that motor racing would have been stopped for ever, not only there but probably throughout Spain. It would have affected the status of motor racing internationally because new countries are unlikely to start motor racing if they feel they are going to put spectators to risk. It is difficult enough to get governments or local authorities to put up money for new or improved circuits and expand the sport into new countries. You have to give motor racing the prestige of a modern, responsible business if it is to increase in the way that everyone who is seriously connected with it wants, and if it is to reach enthusiasts in places where at the moment it does not. Lots of new places will want to run motor races so long as it can be promoted as a prestige operation, or a holiday attraction, not something spectators will avoid for fear of being mown down by a racing car.

The £25,000 or so which the Spanish authorities spent making Montjuich safe was a creditable investment to motor racing worldwide.

7.

Monte Carlo, the Monaco Grand Prix

Monte Carlo, May 18th, 1969. 1.95 miles to the lap, race distance 80 laps, 156.33 miles. The track climbs into Monte Carlo, past the Casino and back down to the harbour side in a spectacular series of sharp corners. It emerges on to the quay side from a tunnel and sweeps along the sea front to a sharp hairpin bend, then back, past the pits and up the hill again. Because of the narrowness and the twisty nature of the track, which is based on the normal roads of the Principality of Monaco, the number of starters is limited to 16. In 1969 there were only seven finishers. The lap record stood at 1.28.1 (79.85 mph) to the credit of Richard Attwood (BRM) from 1968, when he was second to Graham Hill (Lotus-Ford). The starting grid was as follows:

Stewart (Matra-Ford) 1.24.6		**Amon** (Ferrari) 1.25.0	
	Beltoise (Matra-Ford) 1.25.		**Hill** (Lotus-Ford) 1.25.8
Siffert (Lotus-Ford) 1.26.0		**Surtees** (BRM) 1.26.0	
	Ickx (Brabham-Ford) 1.26.3		**Brabham** (Brabham-Ford) 1.26.4
Courage (Brabham-Ford) 1.26.4		**Attwood** (Lotus-Ford) 1.26.5	
	McLaren (McLaren-Ford) 1.26.7		**Hulme** (McLaren-Ford) 1.26.8
Oliver (BRM) 1.28.4		**Rodriguez** (BRM) 1.30.5	
	Moser (Brabham-Ford) 1.30.5		**Elford** (Cooper-Maserati) 1.32.8

The result was:

1st Graham Hill (Lotus-Ford) 1 hour 56 mins. 59.4 sec. 80.18 mph.

2nd Piers Courage (Brabham-Ford) 1 hour 57 mins. 16.7 sec.

3rd Jo Siffert (Lotus-Ford) 1 hour 57 mins. 34.0 sec.

4th Richard Attwood (Lotus-Ford) 1 hour 57 mins. 52.3 sec.

5th Bruce McLaren (McLaren-Ford) 79 laps

6th Denny Hulme (McLaren- Ford) 78 laps

7th Vic Elford (Cooper-Maserati) 74 laps.

Fastest lap, Jackie Stewart 1.25.1, 82.67 mph. (lap 16)

World Championship points after Monte Carlo: 1st Jackie Stewart 18 points. 2nd Graham Hill 15 points. 3rd Bruce McLaren 10 points. 4th Denny Hulme 8 points. 5th Jo Siffert 7 points. 6th Piers Courage 6 points. 7th Jean-Pierre Beltoise 5 points. 8th Richard Attwood 3 points 9th John Surtees 2 points. 10th Jacky Ickx 1 point.

I look forward to Monte Carlo every spring. It would be strange not to. Apart from being a very challenging race track it has a unique charm. When you get out of the aircraft at Nice and drive along the Riviera to Cap Ferrat and Beaulieu and Monaco in the sunshine, past all those beautiful places it is very exciting. You drive up the hill, which is really the circuit, park in front of the Hotel de Paris and are greeted like royalty by the staff as though you had been a constant visitor there for years.

Monte Carlo has so much to offer. There is Rampoli's, The Pirate, Cesar's, - great places. One of the things I enjoy most about being a racing driver is that it enables me to enjoy good restaurants and the best hotels throughout the world. Monte Carlo has good discotheques and of course the Tip Top Bar, it is a complete little place where everyone who is in town for the Grand Prix stays within easy reach of one another. If they are not in the Hermitage or the Paris, they are probably in the Metropole or on a yacht in the harbour, all nearly within walking distance. You hardly need to use a car; you can even walk to the pits.

Monte Carlo always seems to attract the most glamorous people. It is the start of the Riviera season; the Cannes Film Festival has just finished or is still on; the jet set is all there, and this gives off a wonderful ambiance that I do not think you could find at any other racetrack in the world.

I like to arrive a couple of days early at Monte Carlo just to absorb a little of the atmosphere. This year I took an early flight from Geneva after Jo Bonnier's annual party. He holds it at his home almost entirely with motor racing people who are on their way to Monaco from another race, in 1968 for example it was the 1,000 kms Nürburgring sports car event. It is a great party. There was another one when I reached Monaco on the evening of the first practice day. This was Louis Chiron's seventieth birthday party. Louis is a wonderful character, really a part of motor racing and in a sense, we were all sorry that he is not starting races at Monte Carlo any more, although we felt sure he was going to be run down one of these years.

Chiron's race starts were hilarious affairs only rivalled by those of 'Toto' Roche at Rheims. Wearing a blazer, light trousers, and a checked cap which he throws to the ground in moments of stress, Chiron has an animated way of telling you anything, with his arms going like a windmill. He even shouts at you when you are roaring past the pits in your racing car. It is quite unintelligible of course but Louis did not seem happy unless he was hoarse by race day. His starts were precarious to say the least. You felt sure you were going to take him up round St Devote on the bonnet one year, but by 1969 they felt he had served his apprenticeship, and it was time for him to teach the trade to someone else.

I went to his party which was a super affair in the Pirate with Fangio and one of his closest friends Fima Ruchman from Rome. It was a great thrill for me to be driven on the road by Fangio. I had never been in a car with him before and he drove Helen and me to Menton. It was a Mercedes Benz 280 SE and Helen was vastly amused to find me so elated because I was being driven by someone whom I had admired so much. I used to be one of the kids who crowded round for his autograph.

It was quite an occasion. Fangio drove with such polish in the same sort of slumped position he had when he used to drive racing cars, the same way of holding the wheel, the same almost casual air but with everything just right. He drove smoothly and quickly and when corners came, he just seemed to lower one shoulder and the car went round, it was hardly like steering at all.

Fangio is a magnetic sort of man with the most expressive eyes I have ever known. He has a great presence, and he is a great diplomat for motor racing, an ambassador who is above and beyond all the other motor racing 'greats', even Moss and Jimmy Clark. I do not believe that anyone had all the commodities for motor racing that Fangio had - and still seems to have. You can tell when Fangio is around because he gets more attention than Graham and Jochen and me and Ickx and everyone else put together, which is as it should be because Fangio is the Grand Master of our business and everyone in motor racing knows it.

Owing to the use of public roads, special arrangements have to be made for practice at Monaco. The roads are closed for the racing cars early in the morning, adding to the exciting build-up for the race.

Just before practice began, a hastily convened committee of the CSI and the AC de Monaco decided that we were not going to be allowed to use aerofoils. The reason was clearly the near tragedy at Barcelona. Now, Ken Tyrrell knows his rule book. He also knew, as I did, that the decision had been arrived at from the proper motives, but at the wrong time. Ken protested that while banning wings was all right, given time to make the cars to suit, a sudden decision like this could have unlooked-for side effects on existing cars designed specifically for wings, like our Matra MS 80.

Ken pointed out that the regulations made provisions against just such precipitate decisions as this. It just could not be done without the statutory six months' notice, or the Monaco Grand Prix automatically lost its World Championship status. It would be all right to run the race but it would clearly

be a handicap to some runners who might suffer more than others from the loss of their wings and therefore affect their position in the World Championship through no fault of their own. UNLESS we were given time to digest the decision and make adjustments to the cars before the next race.

The whole operation was symptomatic of the CSI's inability to govern motor racing. They had known about wings for a very long time, long before the Barcelona accident, and yet they had never done anything about them. They all knew the date of Monaco and they all knew that Monaco exaggerated the dangers of wings coming off owing to the nature of the circuit and the closeness of spectators. But they had waited for nearly two weeks after Barcelona had

Above: Helen timing Jackie.

Left: The fruits of victory.

Worried faces in the Matra International pit.

Jackie Stewart has tea.

apparently confirmed the risk, before they could be bothered to take a decision about wings. They waited until Paul Frère pointed out the dangers on the very day of practice for the race.

We were not the only people who had a car with the correct springs, dampers, ground clearance and ride height for use with wings. Certainly, we could change these things, but not right there in the garage at Monte Carlo at a few hours' notice. Jack Brabham and Bruce McLaren had just spent something in the region of £800 to £1,200 making new wings between Barcelona and Monte Carlo. Instead of saying at Barcelona, even informally, 'Look, we are thinking of taking a decision to ban wings, halt development of new ones meantime.' They just came along on the first day of practice saying, 'No wings. Get your wings off.'

So, Ken showed them the rule book and said that we were not prepared to take ours off. There was no argument, no scene, he just told them he was not going to do it and he was quite right, whether anyone else was prepared to do it or not. The CSI had to go and get their heads together to see if he was right and of course he was.

Later that afternoon, the constructors were summoned to meet the organisers. Colin Chapman unfortunately was at Indianapolis and Dick Scammell felt he did not have the authority to vote the way he thought Colin would vote, even though Graham Hill was against taking the wings off at such short notice. Ken and Jack Brabham agreed, but the constructors and the CSI and the organisers over-ruled the dissenters and off the wings had to come willy-nilly.

What the fracas had shown however was the weakness of the CSI, and through it the FIA in a crisis, or at any other time for that matter. They had had some bad publicity over the change from 7 litre to 3 litre sports cars and here they were doing something in a matter of hours that the rules said they could not do except with six months' notice. I agree that the six months could have been shortened in the interests of safety, but not ignored entirely. There was certainly no excuse for doing nothing for the two weeks between the two races, indicating to me that the CSI is composed mainly of dear old men who are just not in touch with modern motor racing. Even the British representative could not be found in Monte Carlo for this special meeting. The only exception to the rule was the President of the CSI, Maurice Baumgartner with whom, although I disagreed, I had to admire because at least he was trying to do the right thing.

The root of the trouble of course was that the authorities had allowed wings to grow unnecessarily. They had not kept up with the problem and imposed limits when they had gone beyond the point of safety. They had just smiled weakly and hoped that if they ignored it the whole ghastly problem would just disappear.

While I'm on about safety, it is worth saying that they are going to need to do something about the pits at Monte Carlo. They are on an island like the central reservation of a motorway, so that you sit with racing cars passing in front of you and a few feet away behind you. We have insisted on barriers in front of the pits at every other circuit, but it is just not on at Monaco because the road is too narrow. A car going out of control here could be disastrous for the people in the pits and the fact that they are being passed in both directions multiplies the risk. It looks as though something will need to be built where the tribune by the swimming pool is at the moment and the tribune erected elsewhere.

Wings or no wings, Stewart was fastest in practice on 15th, 16th and 17th May at Monte Carlo. Chris Amon surprised many of his opponents by coming next with the V12 Ferrari and sharing the front row of the 2-2-2 starting grid which the narrowness of the track requires. Jackie's times were 1.24.9 with wings, and 1.24.6 without wings, so it looked as though the wing argument lost some of its point.

We had no axe to grind in the wing controversy. We were fastest with them, and we were fastest without them but the times we achieved the first day were nothing like those which would have been achieved by the end of the weekend because the track was new. Every year at Monte Carlo it takes a day or so to scrub the track in, because in some parts it is quite dusty and has no bite to it. Similarly, you need to treat the first lap or two of the race with respect because the dust comes back in a limited way every night, particularly down on the

Victory lap after a Formula 2 race in a Ford Capri.

Start of the British Grand Prix.

Stewart nearing the end of the British Grand Prix.

waterfront near the Chicane. The surface here can change quite a lot from day to day. Of all the tracks I know, I go slower on my first lap at Monte Carlo than anywhere else.

Cautious or not, Jackie led into the first corner from Chris Amon who remained behind him until the Ferrari's differential broke on lap 16, by which time Jackie was 11 seconds ahead. By the 20th lap he had 30 seconds lead on Graham Hill (Lotus-Ford) who was followed by Beltoise (Matra-Ford), Ickx (Brabham-Ford), and Courage (Brabham-Ford) who were to have an epic battle in the closing stages of the race.

I was travelling very quietly, using the minimum amount of road, the minimum revs, changing gear gently because I knew Monaco to be hard on transmissions. Going down to the waterfront just before the tunnel I was not even using the little bit of pavement you can sometimes employ to gain the odd tenth of a second, because there was a tiny jerk to the transmission when you dropped off the low kerb. Then the drive shaft coupling broke. The car slowed going into the tunnel and I freewheeled down the little hill into the escape road just past the Chicane. I got out of the car, switched everything off and ran along the quayside until I reached the Tabac Comer, went up the steps and through the spectator enclosure and back to the pits, hoping Ken might bring in Jean-Pierre for me to have a go with his car. I did not realise that Jean-Pierre had suffered a similar fate a couple of laps earlier.

Unfortunately, we had had a bad load of universal couplings. It was not a case of ill-treatment or anything like that, it was just a bad batch we had obtained and both cars broke them. Of course, we had to get the bad lot at Monte Carlo ...

All I could do was wander down to the hairpin and watch Graham Hill win his fifth Monaco Grand Prix. It was a disappointment. Great for Graham of course because he was only three points behind me again. The post-race party and going to the Tip Top Bar that night were compensation, however. It is a great race to win because you can have such a celebration; or lose because it is such an easy place to get over the disappointment quickly.

8.

Spa -Safety

If the Belgian Grand Prix had been run in 1969 this chapter would have dealt with it. But there was no Belgian Grand Prix. It was cancelled because the organisers would not agree to certain safety precautions considered essential by most of the drivers and the constructors. There was pressure from the Belgian authorities and the insurance companies to make the Spa circuit, the fastest road racing track in the world, safer for both drivers and spectators.

After Monaco I went fishing. I had three days of complete relaxation and leisure at Aberlour on a three-mile stretch of the Spey, my father has been fishing for 30 years. The salmon were not so plentiful this year, but I flew up with Chris Irwin in his Cessna 310 and met up with a few friends at the Aberlour Hotel. My father joined us, we flew him back in Chris's aircraft, the first time father had flown in anything so small. There was a low cloud base most of the way to Glasgow, but he enjoyed it. I think though, that he's still not too sure about wee aeroplanes.

The highlight of the fishing was caught by the crew who had been making a film about me over the year. You could stand there for months watching somebody fishing and not see him catch anything, but this bunch was on the spot when I brought in a great 20-pound salmon. It was a good fish.

Spa should have been on June 8th. There was never any doubt that it is a circuit of many dangers. It is composed of normal-width roads. Speeds are very high indeed, with no protection at all for the drivers, the cars, or the spectators. It is basically unchanged except for surface improvements and the elimination of one corner, since the 1930s. In wet weather it is lethal, with enormous risk of aquaplaning - the point where you are going so fast the tyres skip across the puddles and you lose touch with the road. Also, the circuit is 8 miles long and local conditions being what they are, it can be raining on one part and dry on another as happened in 1966 when I had my only serious accident.

The organisers, the Royal Automobile Club de Belgique, were uncooperative from the beginning. We, that is the Grand Prix Drivers Association (GPDA), had asked for the start time to be flexible, that is to say in the case of bad weather, things could be rearranged. If it looked like rain in the afternoon, we wanted the race in the morning. Or if it was wet in the morning, we wanted it put off until the weather cleared.

They refused this. First, they said there was the problem of television. We worked that one out with the help of the television people and we could have overcome it. Next, they said there was a possibility of a Royal visit to the race. We did not want to minimise the importance of royalty coming to see a motor race, but frankly we felt safety considerations transcended that, and I have certainly never met any royalty who wanted to see anyone hurt on their account.

Their final argument was really absurd and showed us that they simply were quite inflexible on the subject. They said that the commissaires and the marshals and the spectators in Belgium were accustomed to a three-hour break for lunch and would not like their lunch interrupted if it was suddenly decided to run the motor race. Well, if people rate life and safety that lightly they are just not responsible enough to be running anything.

Everyone realises the dangers at Spa. It has natural hazards that guarantee disaster if a car goes off the road. The lap speed is over 150 mph which includes a 20-mph hairpin bend. Disregarding this, you can imagine that for most of the circuit you are averaging something like 165 mph. Monza is approaching the same sort of speed but there you have safety precautions and the weather is a lot more consistent than it is at Spa.

I went to Belgium on behalf of the GPDA and reported back at Silverstone in March. The decision that Spa was going to be too dangerous to race on was almost unanimous, particularly in view of the intransigence of the organisers who would not make any concessions on safety at all. The only case they had was that we were asking for too many safety precautions and drivers in the past had not asked for anything like them.

Additionally, they claimed they had cost problems. They would need to put barriers up on land that did not belong to them and the local government did not see why they should pay just to help motor racing out of a difficulty.

Since we have started asking for improved safety measures the only people who have been critical of us have often been closely connected with motor racing. If you discuss it with people outside motor racing, they wonder what all the trouble is about. It is normal in almost any field of human activity, industry, travel, the home, roads, and any sport it seems except motor racing to make as much progress as you can in the field of safety. But many of those close to the problem do not seem to see it this way.

Tracks have been making money over the years. It stands to reason they must have because they could not otherwise have been running for all this time. It is my contention that money made in motor racing is not directed back into it the way it would be in any other business enterprise. It has not been used as it should to improve the facilities, and by that I mean not only the safety arrangements, but spectator amenities, the paddock, garage installations and permanent buildings for the press and race officials.

On the particular question of Spa we brought the constructors into a meeting at Silverstone, which showed they felt much the same about it as the drivers. I began to feel I had said enough about Spa but my views received very vocal support from Jack Brabham and his designer Ron Tauranac. Ken did not want to say too much lest he was thought to be merely echoing my feelings and indeed he helped to put the other side of the case on principle. It became quite plain that the constructors agreed with us and a letter was sent to the Belgian club asking for some minimum requirements including a delayed start in the case of rain.

There was no undertaking from the organisers to meet these points but just as a big row was brewing, the insurance problem cropped up and that sealed the fate of the 1969 Belgian Grand Prix.

The Government insisted on unlimited cover for spectators at sporting events in Belgium and the Belgian insurance companies would not cover the Grand Prix. It was perhaps as well that the drivers alone were not responsible for enforcing a ban. Yet it was certainly a good thing that a stand was taken, if only to show that unless organisers were prepared to accept a responsibility to keep their tracks in good safe condition and improve upon them in the light of increased knowledge, there are bodies that care enough to race only where minimum standards obtain.

It must be realised that until there is some alternative expert organization, the GPDA will remain the body of people who know most about circuit safety. If the drivers feel it necessary to put a safety barrier up, the organisers ought to take their word for it. No one is yet more knowledgeable on the subject than the Grand Prix driver largely because he is the one who has to live with it. He knows what a car feels like when it goes out of control. He knows how far it can go. Not many people reading this book can understand what an 1,100 lb car travelling at 140 mph can do.

Grand Prix drivers are not only trying to make things safe for themselves. All these circuits that we race on for the World Championship are used for other types of racing. Other drivers are going to benefit from our experience. There are Formula 3 drivers racing on these tracks who are very new. They must have the chance of making mistakes - and they will make mistakes, we· have all made them at one time or another - but they must have the chance of making them and staying alive.

Anyone serving an apprenticeship will make great big errors and although you must accept a certain amount of hazard in motor racing, there is no need to preserve dangers that can kill people. That is to say there is no need to refuse to remove dangers that can kill people. You must give these young drivers the chance to learn by their experience and not get killed the first time they blunder.

Motor racing must show itself to be responsible enough to plan for its own risks. It does not need much imagination to see what would happen following another disaster like Le Mans in 1955. As it was, several governments banned racing for ever as a direct result of that. After the tragic Mille Miglia of 1957 even such a keen motor racing country as Italy was not long in banning races on public roads because they had been seen to be dangerous. There are opponents of motor racing, even on closed circuits with safety barriers and spectator fences who would like to see it banned for one reason or another, and if the people who are connected with it fail to ensure that every possible precaution is taken, these opponents will have their way. Track racing could become outlawed just as road racing was.

This is one area where the press sometimes disappoints me. Mostly, the attention drivers receive from the press is welcome. Generally, I get on well with journalists, they are a vital part of motor racing, and they are going to play a bigger part in the future. I enjoy the press very much - they are a group with a great sense of humour. But there are one or two, a tiny minority who write about drivers boycotting a Grand Prix and imply we are spoiled or cowards and sometimes I get a little impatient.

They do not enjoy writing about racing drivers being killed and while one respects their right to be critical, it is hard to understand anyone who thinks that Grand Prix drivers are a lot of cowards just because they do not much enjoy the idea of racing under conditions they consider unsafe. Drivers should be given a chance to race safely. I see this very clearly because I am the one behind the wheel. I am the one that loses control. I am the one who makes mistakes.

I do make mistakes, quite often. Just as journalists may forget to re-wind their camera or forget their notebook. But these mistakes can be rectified, racing drivers' mistakes at 140 mph are something else. I do not think I am a particularly brave man. But there is a different mentality between me driving at an average of 150 mph round Spa and a man who is telling me I am a coward and ought not to be motor racing if I cannot do it without something being removed from the trackside, or a barrier put up somewhere.

People do not know what it feels like to be at 150 mph other than on a straight test track somewhere. My job is to race. And if I can drive a racing car fast enough to win a Grand Prix or win the World Championship, I think that those few critical journalists must accept that I am not a coward or have insufficient skill or ability for these circuits. They would be critical of me for going slowly and talking so much about safety possibly. But until that happens, I submit that they have no case.

Helen Stewart and Nina Rindt at the French Grand Prix.

It might disappoint those who claim that Nuvolari or Caracciola or Fangio never complained to know that Fangio thinks Spa too dangerous to race on today. He said that to me two nights before the Italian Grand Prix when we had dinner in the Villa d'Este in Como. Fangio is sensible enough to realise that things are changing all the time. Journalists are not using the same cameras they used ten years ago and we are not using the same cars. Things change and the modern way to go about motor racing or anything else is to introduce as much safety into it as you possibly can. Those who criticise may well continue to do so, but more and more they will appear to be merely eccentrics.

The question of getting paid to do something that is dangerous does not come into the argument at all. I do not feel I am paid for taking risks. I am paid because it is the opinion of those who are paying me that I am likely to win races. They are paying me for skill or ability, not for the risks I am taking. There are lots of youngsters who would willingly take the same risks, but that would

Jackie Stewart and Jochen Rindt.

not necessarily make them worth my pay cheque. In time one of them will be able to outdo my skill I have no doubt and immediately will become worth more than me to my entrant or whoever I am driving for. Until then I feel I am better value to whoever I am driving for when I take the professional attitude of doing my job in the safest way possible because the chances are then that I will be able to race longer and more efficiently. It is as stupid to ignore the possibilities of safety barriers, or roll-over bars, or fire extinguishers as it would be to race without a crash helmet.

9.

Zandvoort, the Dutch Grand Prix

Zandvoort, Holland, June 21st, 1969. 2.61 miles to the lap, race distance 90 laps, 234.9 miles. The track lies in sand dunes on the Dutch coast near Haarlem. There were 15 starters in 1969 and 10 cars finished. The lap record stood to lckx in a Formula 2 car largely because the 1968 Formula 1 race was run in the rain. Ickx's time was 1.27.9 sec. a speed of 106.7 mph. The winner in the wet 1968 race was Stewart, his first with the Grand Prix Matra. he starting grid for 1969 was as follows:

Hill (Lotus-Ford) 1.22.01		**Stewart** (Matra-Ford) 1.21.14		**Rindt** (Lotus-Ford) 1.20.85
	Ickx (Brabham-Ford) 1.22.85		**Amon** (Ferrari) 1.22.69	
Brabham (Brabham-Ford) 1.23.10		**Hulme** (McLaren-Ford) 1.23.07		**McLaren** (McLaren-Ford) 1.22.87
	Siffert (Lotus-Ford) 1.23.94		**Courage** (Brabham-Ford) 1.23.36	
Oliver (BRM) 1.25.11		**Surtees** (BRM) 1.25.07		**Beltoise** (Matra-Ford) 1.24.44
	Elford (McLaren-Ford) 1.28.47		**Moser** (Brabham-Ford) 1.26.50	

The result was:

1st Jackie Stewart (Matra-Ford) 2 hours 6 mms. 42.08 sec 110.4 mph.

2nd Jo Siffert (Lotus-Ford) 2 hours 7 mins. 06.60 sec

3rd Chris Amon (Ferrari) 2 hours 7 mins. 12.59 sec

4th Denny Hulme (McLaren-Ford) 2 hours 7mins. 19.24 sec

5th Jacky Ickx (Brabham-Ford) 2 hours 7 mins. 19.75 sec

6th Jack Brabham (Brabham-Ford) 2 hours 7 mins. 52.89 sec

7th Graham Hill (Lotus-Ford) 88 laps

8th Jean-Pierre Beltoise (Matra-Ford) 87 laps

9th John Surtees (BRM) 87 laps

10th Vic Elford (McLaren-Ford) 84 laps

Fastest lap: Stewart, 1 min 22.94 sec 113.08 mph.

Championship points after Zandvoort :

1st Stewart 27 points. 2nd Hill 15 points. 3rd Siffert 13 points 4th Hulme 11 points. 5th McLaren 10 points. 6th Courage 6 points. 7th Beltoise 5 points 8th Amon 4 points. 9th Attwood 3 points equal Ickx 3 points. 11th Surtees 2 points. 12th Brabham 1 point.

The Dutch Grand Prix is not a very glamorous event. You never get excited in Holland because the crowd seems stolid and unemotional. Zandvoort is a little seaside town, a holiday resort where you sit on the beach, in a wicker chair with a high back to keep the wind off and wrapped in blankets to keep out the cold. If the sun is shining it is probably still cold because of the wind off the sea.

Even the track is somewhat nondescript. It was built amongst the dunes which means there is a perpetual carpet of sand blown onto the road. This acts like a layer of tiny ball bearings and can be most unpleasant to drive on. The trouble is its inconsistency. You can go to Zandvoort on three separate days and have a 5 second difference in your times each day depending on the condition of the track. It varies with the direction of the wind and the dryness of the air and the consequent freedom of the sand to move, making Zandvoort unsatisfactory for serious testing.

Stewart leads from the hill at Monza.

Matra mechanic gives Stewart a pit signal at Clermont Ferrand.

Jacky Ickx takes the winner's garland after his win in the German Grand Prix.

It used to be a good test track, but the cars are so fast now that the corners are too close together for accurate evaluations. Once one of the safest tracks, it now lags behind those which have kept up with increasing speeds and the advances which have taken place in safety knowledge.

John Hugenholz, the man in charge of Zandvoort is one of the world's leading track designers, largely because he is one of the few people who has studied the subject with much care. He likes link fencing beside the track, with which I agree because it minimises the damage to a car that goes off the road. Armco barriers are fairly hard things to hit, and they wrench wheels off - they stop the car abruptly. But chain link fences collect the car, wrap it up and cushions the accident.

John loves Zandvoort so much that he sometimes overlooks its shortcomings. For example, he feels his responsibilities stop at the edge of the track. He will not put up kerbs to stop drivers putting a wheel over the edge of the road to gain an advantage on a corner. In time a hole develops at the edge of the track with the risk that the bump is going to break a suspension arm or damage a tyre. John feels the holes should be left as a deterrent to keep drivers from going over the edge. I feel the holes ought to be filled in or a low kerb built to take away the hazard. The kerb would be sufficient deterrent anyway.

The corners, 'round the back' are probably the most difficult part of Zandvoort. This is a series of bends, first left, then three right handers, another left, and a slow loop on to the straight. They used to be interesting in the days of the 1½ litre cars. You could glance at the rev counter or perhaps the oil pressure gauge between the comers. The tyres were narrow and you could drift through the bends.

Nowadays with wider cars you cannot smooth out Sbends so easily and with the 3 litre's acceleration you are into the next comer before you have completed the last one. I use top gear for these corners at between 8,000 and 8,500 rpm which is somewhere between 150 and 160 mph. You take them in one long manouevre, the car has a cornering force on it all the time. The result is a very critical part of the track which can largely dictate your lap speed, so this is the part of the track that you set the car up for.

During practice drivers carry out a sort of chassis-tuning, a series of adjustments to the suspension by damper and anti-roll bar settings, different spring rates and the like, which provides the optimum handling for each different circuit. The driver amends a car to suit himself. It is a highly individual operation for which they all have their own criteria, a process known as 'setting-up' a car.

Setting-up for these S-bends is very important. The trouble is Zandvoort's inconsistency. You can have a car that understeers or runs wide on corners in practice, but oversteers, or tightens up the corners in the race. The track surface can change within the day.

I had set the car up for the 1969 race with fairly neutral characteristics but on race day it had more oversteer than I could handle, and I just had to go slower. Jochen was a little quicker in practice than I, a fraction under three tenths of a second, which I felt I could make up. In the race, however, the car just would not handle satisfactorily. It was a different car altogether. It slid too much on corners and would not go round them with the precision I had tried to arrange during practice.

The situation in the race was critical. A racing driver must recognise his own limitations. He must be analytical enough to know why his performance may be below par. This is where professional approach and experience counts.

When you are losing ground, you must quickly assemble your thoughts. It is no use trying to drive the car into the ground, using more revs, or holding on to gears between corners where you ought to be changing them. It is no use going deeper into corners before braking, and getting ragged, or exceeding your own personal limit and making mistakes. This is where the Grand Prix driver has to be honest with himself, more honest than in any other situation I know. If you think that either your car or you are not up to staying with an opponent, then you must resist the temptation to try. You have got to know the instant you begin overreaching either your own or the car's limits and slow down. It is easier to go on chasing but you run the risk of making a mistake and bending the car or bursting an engine.

This was the situation I found myself in during the Dutch Grand Prix and I realised I was going to have to play it a little bit cool, go as fast as I could (and I was still pulling away from the opposition), but I was not keeping up with Jochen. He was taking almost half a second a lap off me. It was not possible to remain at that pace and so I did slacken off because it was a 90-lap race, a long way to go.

The start was quite exciting. I was between the two Lotuses, Jochen on pole position and Graham on the left of the front row. I made an indifferent start together with Jochen. Graham was quickest off the line and was ahead at the first corner. Then Jochen tried to overtake Graham up the inside and their cars touched. I sat behind watching and thinking that given reasonable luck they would shortly have each other off the road and on to the grass.

Graham took the advantage and led but the same thing happened on the second lap. They went into Tarzan Corner, Jochen on the grass on the inside, and Graham on the outside, all crossed up. They were getting their wheels mixed up with each other's and were both on opposite lock yet somehow synchronising to get out of the corner again. At the beginning of the third lap Jochen overtook Graham under braking going into the Tarzan, but it really was a scary move and I felt then that if I was patient, I would probably gain a place or two following some incident. I too had trouble getting past Graham and by then Jochen had pulled out an advantage.

He was clearly gaining, and I decided to ease off a fraction. I would have had to overstretch something to keep up, owing to how badly the car was handling. I felt that perhaps Jochen was still liable to tire because the effects of his Barcelona accident had not worn off and I knew that there was always the possibility of a breakdown with the whole race distance ahead of us.

The picture changed dramatically when Jochen's car did break down. A drive shaft coupling disintegrated at speed as he passed the pits, the pieces went showering all over the road and one hit Teddy Mayer who was in the McLaren pit. Jochen coasted to a stop, very disappointed. He was not very pleased with Colin Chapman at the time. They had been having words about something and he said, 'What do you think? That car disintegrated right in front of Chapman's eyes, bits all over the place and not one piece hit him.'

Jackie led for the remainder of the race. It was a tiring event, the worse for him because he had a bout of 'flu coming on and had a few days off on his return to Geneva. One significant innovation at Zandvoort was the arrival of four-wheel drive. There were two cars with this arrangement, one a Lotus driven by Graham Hill in practice, the other the Matra MS 84.

I had driven the four-wheel drive car previously that month and found it a little slower than the conventional car. We still suspected it might be better in the wet, but it was more difficult to drive, and the steering was rather heavy. It was better insofar as it was more forgiving, it allowed you certain liberties in some corners. It was certainly an improvement on the faster corners where it held its line particularly well, but contrary to expectation it was rather unmanageable on slow corners. This we proved by Ken timing me on the slow part of Zandvoort which is from the braking point at the end of the straight, round the Tarzan, through the sharp Hunzerug behind the pits, and then over the top of the hill. I was slower here in the four-wheel drive car than in the two-wheel drive one, but this was an 'interim' car at the very beginning of its development. It had a tubular frame so that the engineers could change their minds easily although it still resembled the shape of the two-wheel drive MS80.

In terms of results, the 1969 season was inconclusive for four-wheel-drive.

10.

Clermont-Ferrand, the French Grand Prix

Clermont-Ferrand, France, July 6th, 1969. 5.005 miles to the lap, race distance 38 laps, 190.19 miles. The Charade circuit comprises closed public roads in the Auvergne with 51 hilly corners. There were 13 starters in 1969 all but one of which, in the absence of BRM, had Ford-Cosworth engines. Ten cars finished the race. The lap record was held by Jim Clark in a 1½ litre Lotus-Climax at 3.18.9, a speed of 90.59 mph. The starting grid was as follows:

Stewart (Matra-Ford) 3.00.6		**Hulme** (McLaren-Ford) 3.02.4	
	Rindt (Lotus-Ford) 3.02.5		**Ickx** (Brabham-Ford) 3.02.6
Beltoise (Matra-Ford) 3.02.9		**Amon** (Ferrari) 3.04.2	
	McLaren (McLaren-Ford) 3.05.5		**Hill** (Lotus-Ford) 3.05.9
Siffert (Lotus-Ford) 3.06.3		**Elford** (McLaren-Ford) 3.08.0	
	Courage (Brabham-Ford) 3.09.		**Miles** (Lotus-Ford) 3.12.8
Moser (Brabham-Ford) 3.14.6			

The result was :

1st Jackie Stewart (Matra-Ford) 1 hour 56 mins. 47.4 sec. 97.71 mph

2nd Jean-Pierre Beltoise (Matra-Ford) 1 hour 57 mins. 44.5 sec

3rd Jacky Ickx (Brabham-Ford) 1 hour 57 mins. 44.7 sec

4th Bruce McLaren (McLaren-Ford) 37 laps.

5th Vic Elford (McLaren-Ford) 37 laps

6th Graham Hill (Lotus-Ford) 37 laps

7th Silvio Moser (Brabham-Ford) 36 laps

8th Denny Hulme (McLaren-Ford) 35 laps

9th Jo Siffert (Lotus-Ford) 34 laps

10th Chris Amon (Ferrari) 30 laps.

Fastest lap, Stewart, 3.02.7, 98.62 mph. **World Championship points** after Clermont-Ferrand: 1st Stewart 36 points. 2nd Hill 16 points. 3rd Siffert 13 points. equal McLaren 13 points. 5th Hulme 11 points. equal Beltoise 11 points. 7th Ickx 7 points. 8th Courage 6 points. 9th Amon 4 points.10th Attwood 3 points. 11th Surtees 2 points. equal Elford 2 points. 13th Brabham 1 point.

Clermont is probably one of the four most difficult tracks in the world. Nürburgring's fourteen miles almost certainly comes first but they are both so complex that an intimate knowledge of them is overwhelmingly important. You can remember the geography of the Nürburgring but there are many things you will never get to know without the experience of say several 1,000 kilometre sports car races there, or a touring car 84-hour marathon.

Clermont is different. You can read all the comers within its five miles with much more accuracy simply because you can get to know them better. The other two top circuits for drivers are Monte Carlo, and Pau, which is used for Formula 2 races. The surface at Clermont is good. There are two very similar places, two comers where the scenery is so alike you have to think out every lap which one you are approaching. Confusion would not be dangerous.

You would be unlikely to have an accident through mistaking one for the other but you could be slower.

We went to Clermont by road from Geneva in the Zodiac along with Jochen and Nina in their Lotus Elan plus 2, which was something of an adventure. First of all, it must be one of the worst roads in France. Jochen insisted we accompany him in case the Lotus did not make the distance. As it was, the passenger door threatened to fall off and Nina nearly travelled with us. She thought Jochen was going to have them off the road because of the bumps. We arrived at the border into France and Jochen found he had no insurance green card and had to buy one on the spot. He can be incredibly disorganised.

There were one or two other incidents. Jochen missed a red light and nearly had a punch-up. Then we went into a tiny cafe at the scruffiest filling station in the whole of France and I left my brief case behind. It was like losing the Crown Jewels. It contained my address book, my money, passport, diary, everything of importance that I carried. It was very careless of me and I was not very optimistic about getting it back. However, I had misjudged French honesty. The proprietor had seen my name on it and handed it over to the local police.

The following day a friend who had come with us from Geneva, Richard Burton, very kindly offered to go back, find the filling station and try to retrieve the case. He is slimly built, has longish hair and wears trendy clothes and when he returned to the village all the local people immediately concluded that this was Jackie Stewart who had returned for his lost property. He dared not let them down because they had all been so excited about the driver of 'their' French Grand Prix car, the Matra, coming to the village and before they would let him leave he had to sign autographs in the police station and the café and they cheered him every place he went. It only needed someone to come in and say he was not Jackie Stewart and he would have been clapped in jail for fraud or something.

We stayed at Royat alongside Clermont, which is supposed to be a health spa and is full of old dears whose dinner tables look like chemists' counters. The hotels are like mausoleums and there is a general air of decrepitude. The hills and the humidity cannot be good for the old souls and I am quite sure that if they went anywhere else in France, they would immediately leap out of their wheel chairs and rejuvenate. I was exhausted in the place after two days and everyone seemed to have tummy upsets. If you are going to feel ill anywhere you will feel ill here. I felt like an old man at Royat and Jochen for one felt sick in his racing car. It was not just the switchback nature of the circuit, or so many lateral changes of direction with quite high cornering forces. Your head gets banged from one side of the cockpit to the other. Jochen still did not seem fully recovered from his Barcelona accident, his equilibrium had not settled down and he wore Piers's spare helmet to try and give him more fresh, cool air round his face instead of the closed-up Bell Star he had adopted.

Clermont turned out to be a copy-book performance by Stewart. He set up the fastest time in each of the three practice periods. He put up good times in the four-wheel drive car which was still in the experimental stage. He led the race from start to finish, lapping at an easy pace three seconds inside his best practice time and included a lap record or two for good measure.

Equally, it was a perfect performance for Ken Tyrrell and Matra International, with their star driver ensuring outright victory and their French number two providing all the excitement in a spectacular duel with Jacky lckx (Brabham Ford), to finish in second place. A Matra one-two in the French Grand Prix, with the crowd's own darling JeanPierre Beltoise giving them their best result for decades was a triumph for Tyrrell. It was before the very eyes of the French Elf petrol concern which sponsored the team, together with the high priests of Matra, who had also put their faith in him.

It was a convincing demonstration to the French. Too convincing perhaps, as events were soon shaping that would result in Stewart having to find another make of car to contest the World Championship of 1970.

You have to go easy during the first few laps at Clermont because it is very important on such a circuit to see signs of any oil trace in good time. It is difficult to see oil which may have been left by the other cars on the first lap with so many blind corners and hills and parts of the road shaded by trees. The sun may not be getting through to glisten on an oil patch so your second lap at

Oulton Park Gold Cup: Stewart leads the field on the first lap.

The Matra about to plunge down into Deer's Leap at Oulton Park.

Crowds thronged to Dunlop caravan, Stewart finds refuge.

Jackie talking to Austin Campbell, Andrew Maconie.

Clermont has to be taken with care too. There was no need to worry this time and the race was uneventful until I came upon skid marks from time to time. These spread out in some corners to places you would never dream a racing car would go in the normal course of events.

There was earth loosened from banks and occasionally I could see photographers talking animatedly and obviously still recovering from an exciting experience. I realised there must be a real dice going on somewhere at the back of the field. Of course, this was Jean-Pierre and Jacky, who were passing and re-passing several times every lap.

My gear ratios were just right, and I was able to keep the revs down to a very comfortable level after Denny had stopped at his pit to repair the suspension. Keeping revs in hand was something I was able to do several times during the season which perhaps had something to do with our engine reliability record. You drive with a lighter throttle and get an easier engine pick-up from low revs instead of merely stamping your foot to the floor, because sometimes you choke it and it does not pick up smoothly. It is possible to eliminate flat spots by applying the throttle progressively, you almost feel your way through the power curve by opening the throttle with a tickle rather than a jab. It is satisfying on a driver's circuit like Clermont to think all this out when you are racing at a gait well within your capacity. You try to control the race, and conserve the car, knowing you have something in hand should the occasion demand.

Ken, of course, could see that the pace was suiting me and while I was getting the revs down from 10,000 to 9,500 and eventually not using much more than 9,000, he hung out a signal which read, 'Use 8,500'. If Ken is in doubt he always says, 'Use 8,500', even though there is no power there. It makes him feel happy, so I nod agreement and keep the revs down every time I pass the pits.

Clermont did not seem to have enough money to put on the Grand Prix. It is a wealthy area, the home of Michelin and industrially prosperous but they seemed to feel the Grand Prix was not worth very much to them. So, it was at least partly their own fault that the entry was rather diminished in numbers. But having now won four out of the season's five Grand Prix races I had no reason to complain about anything.

11.

Silverstone, the British Grand Prix

Silverstone, Northants, July 19th, 1969, 2.927 miles to the lap, race distance 84 laps, 245.96 miles. Former airfield circuit, flat and rather featureless. There were 17 starters and 10 finishers in 1969. The lap record stood to Chris Amon (Ferrari) from the April 1968 Daily Express Trophy meeting with 1.25.1, a speed of 123.82 mph. The starting grid was as follows:

Hulme (McLaren-Ford) 1.21.5		**Stewart** (Matra-Ford) 1.21.2		**Rindt** (Lotus-Ford) 1.20.8
	Amon (Ferrari) 1.21.9		**Ickx** (Brabham-Ford) 1.21.6	
Rodriguez (Ferrari) 1.22.6		**McLaren** (McLaren-Ford) 1.22.6		**Surtees** (BRM) 1.22.21
	Courage (Brabham-Ford) 1.22.9		**Siffert** (Lotus-Ford) 1.22.7	
Oliver (BRM) 1.23.7		**Hill** (Lotus-Ford) 1.23.6		**Elford** (McLaren-Ford) 1.23.3
	Bell (McLaren-Ford) 1.26.1		**Miles** (Lotus-Ford) 1.25.1	
	Beltoise (Matra-Ford) 1.31.2		**Bonnier** (Lotus-Ford) 1.28.2	

Reg Parnell (Racing) had announced they were going to suspend their racing activities in the meantime, releasing Pedro Rodriguez to Ferrari. Derek Bell joined McLaren to drive their experimental four-wheel drive car.

The result was as follows:

1st Jackie Stewart (Matra-Ford) 1hour 55min 55.6sec, 127.25mph

2nd Jacky Ickx (Brabham-Ford) 83 laps, 1hour 56 min 36.1 sec

3rd Bruce McLaren (McLaren-Ford) 83 laps, 1 hour 56 min. 42.5 sec

4th Jochen Rindt (Lotus-Ford) 83 laps.

5th Piers Courage (Brabham-Ford) 83 laps

6th Vic Elford (McLaren-Ford) 82 laps.

7th Graham Hill (Lotus-Ford) 81 laps.

9th Jean-Pierre Beltoise (Matra-Ford) 78 laps.

10th John Miles (Lotus-Ford) 75 laps.

Fastest lap, Stewart, 1.21.3, 129.61 mph.

World Championship points after Silverstone: 1st Stewart 45 points. 2nd McLaren 17 points. 3rd Hill 16 points. 4th Siffert 13 points. equal Ickx 13 points. 6th Hulme 11 points. equal Beltoise 11 points. 8th Courage 8 points. 9th Amon 4 points. 10th Attwood 3 points. equal Rindt 3 points. equal Elford 3 points. 13th Surtees 2 points 14th Brabham 1 point

My relationship with the Mark McCormack organization, with whom I had become associated earlier in the year had now started to bring results in the form of a great deal of work every time I came to Britain. On the way to Silverstone during our stay in London, Helen and I lived in an endless succession of interviews, filming, and telephone calls. We drove Nina Rindt in from the airport, she was going to consult a doctor about a back injury received in an Autocross when Jochen rolled a Mini. We had an Executive Zodiac and going through the traffic on Brompton Road clipped the rear of a Morris Minor Traveller. There was hardly a mark on the other car but considerable damage to mine. Two tanned holidaymakers got out, very cross, announcing that they had driven from the North of England to Spain and then all the way back, 'And now you crash into us when we're almost home.'

I had to apologise and the man turned out to be a lawyer or a magistrate or something, and I was sure there would be all sorts of trouble. I could see headlines, 'RACING DRIVER COLLIDES WITH HOLIDAY COUPLE' or 'JACKIE STEWART TERRORISES LONDON TRAFFIC'. So, we exchanged names and addresses. The man was very nice about it, and of course I was simply John Young Stewart c/o Ford Motor Company, Warley, Brentwood, Essex. Nina meanwhile had gone off in a taxi, having decided that travelling through London with Jackie Stewart at the wheel was much too dangerous.

We stayed near Silverstone with Lord Alexaner Hesketh at Towcester Park along with Helen, Jochen, Nina, Piers, and his wife Sally. Alexander is quite a character. He is quite young and has one of the most beautiful houses in England. We had a helicopter to take us to the circuit and Alexander had his Aston Martin DBS to transport us from the helicopter to the pits. We could not have been better organised.

The Daily Express put up £100 at Silverstone for the fastest lap for every half hour of the final day's practice. Stewart went out in the first session and won the first £ 100 within about three laps. Immediately afterwards he went out with full tanks, using the remainder of the half hour trying out the car with the extra weight. He returned to have the tanks unloaded so that he could again try for some fast times, used the four-wheel drive car to qualify it in case of rain on race day, then won a second £100 in the closing moments of the second half hour.

Somewhere halfway through the third session I went out and had just got down to 1.21s when I came round Woodcote to find a little piece of the concrete kerb had been dislodged. I saw the pieces lying on the road as I approached but the car was committed to the line and there was nothing I could do. At that sort of speed - about 140 mph - the car is finely balanced, right on tiptoe so to speak and if you try to change direction suddenly you have the accident just the same.

The fragments were thrown up by the front wheel. One bit weighed 3 lbs and it must have caught the rear tyre end on because it took almost the entire tread off.

The tyre exploded and the next moment I was spinning through Woodcote. I felt sure I was going straight into the bank at high speed and I had a 'This is going to be a Big One,' feeling. Then I realised I had missed it on the first spin, and I was now going slower. There was a great, jarring thud when we hit the sleeper wall backwards and the front flipped round once again. There was dust and rubber smoke everywhere but no fire.

Almost before the thing stopped, I thought, 'My God, Helen's watching this, my father's watching this, everyone's watching this, it must look terrifying.' So when the car stopped I leapt out, breaking the screen in my anxiety to show them I was all right. It seemed the right thing to do. I also wanted to warn the marshals on the other side of the road about the fragments. Piers Courage went past and threw pieces of my tyre into the air, and I wanted to avoid a repetition of my accident.

The marshals at Woodcote Corner were beside me in a moment, concerned that perhaps I had given myself a bump on the head. In fact, they were convinced that I had given myself a bump on the head because it seemed all I wanted to do was rush across the road in front of the other racing cars. A medical man immediately got a hold of me. I wanted to tell the marshals on the inside of the corner to get that muck swept up and the medical man wanted me to come with him, 'Quietly now Jackie it was a bigger accident than you think.' Eventually we got the message across, and the track was cleared. They were absolutely right of course. Restraining my immediate reactions and check me over were the correct things to do.

The monocoque of my Matra had been damaged quite badly and there was no hope of it being repaired in time for the race. There were relieved cheers from the crowd, and the commentator I believe had been going on about how wonderfully I had controlled the car, which was so much nonsense really. Sometimes you can influence the course of a spin but on this occasion I had absolutely no control over the thing whatsoever. It was virtually on three wheels, its destiny certainly not in my hands.

In a spin like this one you are very busy and you see the earth swapping ends quite clearly and you know you are spinning. Everything goes quiet. You can see the smoke and you know you are heading for a solid bank, but you do not really think you are going to hurt yourself. I do not cringe up except perhaps involuntarily. My shoulder was stiff the next day where I had bumped against the side of the cockpit.

They stopped practice while the wreckage was cleared, and I got into Jean-Pierre's car to go out immediately afterwards. It was clear that my car would never be ready and that I would have to qualify in another car. This was hard luck on Jean-Pierre who was going to have to use the four-wheel drive car but the Championship was at stake and this was how it had to be. Jean-Pierre is a good team member and mmediately offered me his car which was extremely praiseworthy of him.

What was most remarkable about Jackie's performance following the accident was that he went out in Jean-Pierre's car, not having driven it for some time, not being able to sit in it correctly owing to the controls being too far away (Stewart sits relatively close to the steering wheel and pedals) yet within two or three laps was down to 1.21.1 which was a good front-row-of-the-grid time very little slower than what he had done previously. Meanwhile Jochen had collected £200 from the last two sessions without reaching Stewart's best time with his now wrecked car of 1.20.6.

I had completed only a few laps when the doctors called me in. They wanted to give me a full medical check-up in case I was suffering from shock or concussion of any kind, which again was a very sensible precaution. I had not considered it in the hurry to obtain a qualifying time with the other car, but I was not annoyed at being asked to get out and let them poke around to make sure I had no unsuspected injury.

I did not make as swift a start in the race as Jochen. He braked a little earlier than I expected at Copse so I gently nudged him from behind but nobody seemed to notice. It was just a puff of smoke when my front aerofoil hit his rear wheel. The start had been strange. Dean Delamont had jiggled the flag a bit and Jochen and I both false started. Surtees was in the third row, but he did not think twice and by Copse he was in third place behind us.

Jochen and I continued nose to tail for five laps until at Beckets, which is a slowish right hander, I drew alongside. It must have looked a little scary and you need to trust each other implicitly in a move like this. We went round side by side executing a sort of pas de deux which we both enjoyed and exchanged meaningful glances going down Hangar Straight. He beat me into Stowe, the fast right hander at the end of the straight and then I overtook him under breaking the following lap again at Stowe. It was a good dice; we were both enjoying it and both taking advantage of the lead we were pulling out.

Nine laps later he passed me again the same way at Beckets and we went round in convoy, close together for some time thereafter. We had reached a kind of stalemate. Each could just scratch past the other without being able to draw away afterwards, there was no way I was going to take anything off him and no way he was going to pull away from me. But a close scrap would have slowed both of us. It was better to keep station and pull away from the opposition together.

When we came up to lap a bunch of cars around half distance Jochen went through them quickly and made some ground, about 300 yards or thereabouts. My fuel load had decreased sufficiently to allow me to take Club in fourth gear and I began immediately to get under 1.22.0, enabling me to catch up on Jochen. But just as I closed in, a piece of his aerofoil started breaking loose. I drew alongside to point to it because it looked perilously close to the rear tyre. Jochen had seen it too, signalled to me and drove straight up the pit road.

In closing up on Jochen, Jackie set a new record speed on laps 51 and 60, just before Jochen went into his pit on lap 62. Jochen was subsequently delayed by another pit stop for fuel and Jackie had trouble with a malfunctioning petrol feed. One pump would stop working on left hand bends so that in the closing stages of the race he had to switch off the engine going through Abbey Curve, one of the two left hand bends on the circuit. At the finish he was the only car to complete the full distance, having lapped the entire field.

Winning the British Grand Prix had long been an ambition. It had never been a race where I had done well before, which had been a disappointment because I always had people down from Scotland to watch. Somehow, I had always wanted to give them better value for their journey, and I had never been able to. Several motoring journalists who had taken an interest in the early days of my motor racing in Scotland were there, people like Jim McLaren of the Glasgow Herald, Jim Bowman of The Scotsman, Alistair Cameron of the Scottish Express and Malcolm McDougal of the Daily Record and other members of the Association of Scottish Motoring Writers.

My father had at last seen me win a Grand Prix and I think he got as big a thrill from it as he did when my brother Jim did so well in the 1954 grand prix in the Cooper-Bristol. He does not get to as many races although usually watches British races and enjoys them. I felt he was proud when I won at Silverstone and that pleased me.

We went round on the trailer for the lap of honour with some of the Dunlop chiefs. They were happy too because this was on their own doorstep in the Midlands and they so wanted to win. They had brought everyone from the factory that they could, and it was a great occasion. They were all there on the trailer from Bill Bailey who is Director in charge of Dunlop's tyre activities, Dan Keily, and of course Dick Jeffrey, Iain Mills, Alec Meskell, all of them down to Arthur the tyre fitter. It was the complete Dunlop range, and the only missing person was Ken, who turns surprisingly shy whenever anything like that takes place.

A question arose in the press afterwards whether Stewart would have won if Rindt had not dropped out. The Stewart v. Rindt controversy - which is the faster driver, then broke out in earnest. It had been going on for years. The two had battled together in Formula 2 where the verdict went to Rindt in terms of sheer results, but not by as wide a margin as might have appeared. If you consider the races in which they competed on level terms (which leaves out the 1969 season when Stewart's car was already two years old) Rindt had very little advantage although he rarely failed to win a Formula 2 race when Stewart was not present.

By now the friendly but fairly intense rivalry became more noticeable because Rindt had a car which could compete with Stewart's. Up till the end of 1969 there was no conclusive evidence that one was quicker than the other. No race was fought out to a fair finish then or subsequently, but exciting battles between them were often features.

Until any better criteria are established, one must go on the results of the races on which Stewart was certainly concentrating in 1968 and 1969, the World Championship Grands Prix.

12.

Nürburgring, the German Grand Prix

Nürburgring, West Germany, August 3rd, 1969, 14.19 miles to the lap, race distance 14 laps, 198.64 miles The Nürburgring twists and turns like a switchback through the pine covered Eifel Mountains in West Germany. With a reputed 84 left and 80 right-handed corners to the lap the 'Ring is one of the most famous road circuits in

Rindt (Lotus-Ford) 7.48.0		**Stewart** (Matra-Ford) 7.42.4		**Ickx** (Brabham-Ford) 7.42.1
	Hulme (McLaren-Ford) 7.52.8		**Siffert** (Lotus-Ford) 7.50.3	
McLaren (McLaren-Ford) 7.56.5		**Courage** (Brabham-Ford) 7.56.1		**Elford** (McLaren-Ford) 7.54.8
	Beltoise (Matra-Ford) 8.00.3		**Hill** (Lotus-Ford) 7.57.0	
Oliver (BRM) 8.16.2		**Andretti** (Lotus-Ford) 8.15.4		**Bonnier** (Lotus-Ford) 8.35.0

FORMULA 2 GRID

Pescarolo (Matra-Ford F2) 8.14.8		**Cevert** (Techno-F2) 8.13.9		**Servoz-Gavin** (Matra-Ford F2) 8.11.1
	Ahrens (Brabham-Ford F2) 8.23.2		**Westbury** (Brabham-Ford F2) 8.20.0	
Perrot (Brabham-Ford F2) 8.35.4		**Stommelen** (Lotus-Ford F2) 8.28.1		**Attwood** (Brabham-FordF2) 8.24.6

the world. A normal Formula 1 field would look thin, so the Automobilclub von Deutschland arranged a Formula 2 race concurrently with the Grand Prix.

There were 21 starters in the 1969 combined event, 13 Formula 1 and 8 Formula 2 of whom 6 Formula ls ·and 6 Formula 2s finished. The lap record was held by Jackie Stewart in a Matra-Ford Formula 2 at 8 mins. 05.3 sec, a speed of 105.26 mph. The starting grid was as follows:

The result was :

1st Jacky Ickx (Brabham-Ford) 1 hour 49 mins. 55.4 sec 108mph.

2nd Jackie Stewart (Matra-Ford) 1 hour 50 mins. 53.1 sec.

3rd Bruce McLaren (McLaren-Ford) 1 hour 53 mins. 17.0 sec.

4th Graham Hill (Lotus-Ford) 1 hour 53 mins. 54.2 sec.

5th Henri Pescarolo (Matra-Ford F2) 1 hour 58 mins. 06.4 sec. 100.91 mph.

6th Richard Attwood (Brabham-Ford F2) 1 hour 49 mins. 57.1 sec.13 laps.

7th Kurt Ahrens (Brabham-Ford F2) 1 hour 49 mins. 57.4 sec. 13 laps.

8th Rolf Stommelen (Lotus-Ford F2) 1 hour 50 mins. 13.9 sec. 13 laps.

9th Peter Westbury (Brabham-Ford F2) 1 hour 51 mins. 34.5 sec. 13 laps.

10th Xavier Perrot (Brabham-Ford F2) 1 hour 54 mins. 53.1 sec. 13 laps.

11th Jo Siffert (Lotus-Ford) 12 laps classified 5th F.1 although not running at finish.

12th Jean-Pierre Beltoise (Matra-Ford) 12 laps classified 6th F.1 although not running at finish.

Fastest lap Jacky Ickx (Brabham-Ford) 7 mins. 43.8 sec.110.13 mph.

World Championship points after Nürburgring: 1st Stewart 51 points. 2nd Ickx 22 points. 3rd McLaren 21 points. 4th Hill 19 points. 5th Siffert 13 points. 6th Beltoise 11 points equal Hulme 11 points. 8th Courage 8 points. 9th Amon 4 points. 10th Attwood 3 points. equal Elford 3 points. equal Rindt 3 points. 13th Surtees 2 points. 14th Brabham 1 point.

Helen had never been to the Nürburgring, but she came this time. After Silverstone I had allowed that there was a chance, perhaps just a chance I might win the World Championship. There were still ways I could be beaten although the mathematics were beginning to be on my side. Winning this race would have clinched it and Helen wanted to be there if it happened. Every time she came on the winner's dais of a Grand Prix during the season she said, 'That's another one,' and told me my Championship score.

I had always discouraged her from going to the 'Ring because it can be a difficult place for a racing driver's wife. The worst thing about it is the eight-minute wait before your car comes round again. In the event of a breakdown or a small accident, she could have sat in the pits for three quarters of an hour wondering what had happened, with everyone looking the other way and saying maybe it's nothing but all the while wondering. This sort of drama is best avoided. But undaunted, Helen rearranged Margaret Boag, our Nanny's weekend off and came with me.

The first thing was to take the BMW Hubert Hahne had lent me round to remind myself of the track's terrors. The Dunlop fitters always queue up for trips round the Nürburgring and I try to take Ken round just to let him see how he's spending his money but around Adenau Bridge he usually wants to get off. That circuit really is a different world from the passenger's seat; it can scare the living daylights out of you. Dan Gurney once took me round. It was my first time at the 'Ring and it was pretty scary. This year it was my turn to take Mario Andretti, pointing out the roadside references, or the advertising signs where you aim the car.

Driving at the Nürburgring brings out the best in you. It illustrates the competition that the racing driver has at any circuit. I do not simply mean the race, that is something else. I mean the conflicting elements of speed and the track and the car. The driver's job is to arrange things so that they are all working in harmony and in his favour. This is more difficult here than anywhere else in the world.

You must become part of the car and mould yourself into it not merely physically. You can do that with a well-shaped seat and properly laid out controls. You have to mould yourself into the car's personality. Then you must synchronise yourself with speed. This means that instead of rushing down the curves towards the Fox Hole in a mighty blur of colour and trees and hedges and road, you must have the mental faculty of slowing things down. Instead of a meaningless jumble of shapes, you need the ability and the discipline to pick out details. It is rather like a film where you reduce the speed of the frames in front of your eyes. You focus on a point as far down the road as you can see and yet you take everything in. All the features of the scene register in plenty of time to lay the necessary plans for driving round them or past them. Speed in terms of miles per hour becomes almost meaningless provided you are in the correct, receptive state of mind to control its sensations. You have plenty of time to change into top gear, you know you are doing 165 mph all right, but it does not intimidate you. You have time to realise that you are going to lift off the ground here and you will have to hit the apex of a corner early because of the jump the car is taking. You can see clearly enough to say, 'No, I can keep my foot in it till after the bottom of this hill.' Then you know where to lift off and brake and decide to take the left hander in fourth or jump straight from fifth to third without disturbing the car too much.

A Formula 1 car is not much like any other car. Smoothness becomes of paramount importance. There are some places where smoothness is difficult, like Monte Carlo for instance, but even so, the gentler you are with the brakes, the more carefully you apply the power or turn the steering, the quicker you are likely to be. I am sure there is something to be learned from this in driving every sort of car, but it is essential to use the technique in a Formula 1 car. There is no other way.

This smoothness is something I had to culture. It has nothing to do with ability. You have to coax a car into a corner, you cannot go stamping on the brakes. It is in such perfect balance that a sudden movement will upset everything. A Formula 1 car is highly strung and you take it through a corner gently because this is its most painful moment when all the camber angles change and the suspension arms are being wrenched. It is like driving on a knife blade, you simply must keep it on the line you choose for it otherwise you go 'off the edge.'

Some days you feel that you and the car are not talking. You are not tuned into one another. The driver may be off form, everything seems to happen in a rush, you find it difficult to tum on the 'slow-motion camera'. Sometimes you almost feel like a passenger and you are being taken along with the car. IT knows the circuit. Sometimes as a result you over-drive the car and this is when you have to sit down and analyse just why it is behaving this way. You must find out what it has, say too much roll stiffness or too hard springs, and you have to try and describe what is wrong to the engineers and describe it accurately enough for them to make the appropriate adjustments. This is not always easy.

Sometimes you change the anti-roll bar, or perhaps the springs, or the angle of the aerofoil and all of a sudden the car begins to react more pleasantly towards you. It does not rebel. Before adjustment, it might react unexpectedly to a particular bump in the road or behave unpredictably in a comer. It is no use going at it like a rodeo, you have to find out what is wrong and take steps to put it right. You are talking to each other again. It takes both of you to win a motor race.

I do not like to drive a car aggressively. It is tiring and difficult to be forever sliding through comers and have a lot of oversteer, because it is wasting time and not the right way. I prefer to do it more quietly, in a gear higher than perhaps most people would employ, because this way a car is more docile and under more control.

Practice for the German Grand Prix became something of a duel between Stewart and Ickx. The young Belgian, with his enormous fund of experience on the circuit, and his strongly built Brabham matched Stewart's times in bright, sunny weather which contrasted strongly with the fog and rain of the 1968 triumph. Ickx was repeating a feat of his own in 1967 when he drove Ken Tyrrell's Formula 2 Matra, setting a practice time of 8.14.0 that would have put him on the front rank of that Grand Prix grid between Hulme in the RepcoBrabham-V8 and Stewart in the H-16 BRM. The lightweight Matra was certainly at some advantage, but his closest adversary in the same class was the eventual winner of the Formula 2 section that year, Jackie Oliver with 8.34.9 in a Lotus, which would have just gained him the back row of the Formula 1 grid.

Now in 1969 lckx took pole position with 7.42.1. Stewart was next with 7.42.4, a tiny margin at the Nürburgring. Jochen Rindt could not get within five seconds of them.

I got a good start in the race and had a few seconds' lead by the time I got to the Flugplatz. By the end of the first lap, it was 6 seconds, and 11 seconds on the second lap over Jo Siffert. Then the gears began to give trouble. At first, I thought it was me, I thought I had not been putting the gears into mesh properly and they were jumping out, so I became more deliberate when I changed gear. But once or twice they refused to engage at all and I had to miss them occasionally. This did not affect my lap times much at first, but meant they were not improving as the fuel load diminished.

I could now see Jacky Ickx in the mirror and for the next three laps he closed up, which must have been a good spectacle for the crowd. He made one or two efforts to pass and on one occasion at the North Turn dived up inside me with no hope of making the corner. I caught a flash of green out of the corner of my eye as the Brabham slithered out towards the edge of the road so I re-passed on the inside and carried on.

But the Matra was now disabled, and Jacky eventually passed at the South Turn. The gearbox became worse until I was sometimes left with only one gear and there was nothing I could do about catching him. It was all the more annoying because it was so inconsistent. A selector fork had bent and sometimes it seemed the trouble had righted itself, until the next time I changed down through the box for a corner and I would have to jiggle the lever and try to feel it into any gear that would engage. I drove the last couple of laps with third and fifth when I could get them although I managed to remain ahead of Bruce by more than two minutes.

This race brought Ickx from fourth equal place in the Championship into second place behind Jackie. There was, however, no way he could beat Stewart's points before the end of the year even if he had won all the next four races after Germany. The system would have obliged him to discount one of his scores. But Bruce McLaren in third place one point behind Ickx could still catch up. He would need to win all the remaining races with Stewart failing to reach the first six each time but he could have done it

13.

Monza, the Italian Grand Prix

Monza, Italy, September 7th, 1969. 3.57 miles to the lap, race distance 68 laps, 242.95 miles. Lying in fiat country close to Milan, Monza Park has long straights and fast bends. The banked track was no longer used for the Grand Prix.

There were 15 starters and 11 finishers. The lap record was held by Jackie Oliver (Lotus-Ford) at 1 min. 26.5 sec., a speed of 148.69 mph. The starting grid was as follows:

Rindt (Lotus-Ford) 1.25.48		**Hulme** (McLaren-Ford) 3.02.4	
	Stewart (Matra-Ford) 1.25.82		**Courage** (Brabham-Ford) 1.26.48
McLaren (McLaren-Ford) 1.26.48		**Beltoise** (Matra-Ford) 1.26.72	
	Brabham (Brabham-Ford) 1.26.90		**Siffert** (Lotus-Ford) 1.27.04
Hill (Lotus-Ford) 1.27.31		**Surtees** (BRM) 1.27.40	
	Oliver (BRM) 1.28.40		**Rodriguez** (Ferrari) 1.28.47
Moser (Brabham-Ford) 1.28.51		**Ickx** (Brabham-Ford) 1.37.96	
Miles (Lotus-Ford) 1.30.56			

The result was:

1st Jackie Stewart (Matra-Ford) 1 hour 39 mins. 11.26 sec. 146.96 mph.

2nd Jochen Rindt (Lotus-Ford) 1 hour 39 mins. 11.34 sec.

3rd Jean-Pierre Beltoise (Matra-Ford) 1 hour 39 mins. 11.43 sec.

4th Bruce McLaren (McLaren-Ford) 1 hour 39 mins. 11.45 sec.

5th Piers Courage (Brabham-Ford) 1 hour 39 mins. 44.70 sec.

6th Pedro Rodriguez (Ferrari) 66 laps.

7th Denny Hulme (McLaren-Ford) 66 laps.

8th Jo Siffert (Lotus-Ford) 64 laps (not running at finish)

9th Graham Hill (Lotus-Ford 63 laps (not running at finish)

10th Jacky Ickx (Brabham-Ford) 61 laps (not running at finish)

11th John Surtees (BRM) 60 laps.

Fastest lap Jean-Pierre Beltoise, 1 min. 25.2 sec. 150.96 mph.

World Championship points after Monza:

1st Stewart 60 points. 2nd McLaren 24 points. 3rd Ickx 22 points. 4th Hill 19 points. 5th Beltoise 16 points. 6th Siffert 15 points. 7th Hulme 11 points. 8th Rindt 9 points. 9th Amon 4 points. 10th Attwood 3 points. equal Elford 3 points. 12th Surtees 2 points. 13th Brabham 1 point. equal Rodriguez 1 point.

Having won the Oulton Park Gold Cup race as well as Nürburgring it looked as though Jacky lckx was becoming a keen rival in the second half of the season. He could not threaten for the Championship, but he bade strongly for second place and seemed determined to pursue Stewart for all he was worth. Monza proved Ickx's undoing. After a row with his team during practice he started at the back of the grid before retiring with engine trouble.

Racing drivers, like any other sportsmen have a period of adjustment at early stages of their careers. Jacky Ickx appeared to be on this threshold, an important one for his future as a racing driver. He had the ability and the acclaim of being a top driver, and now had to accept their restraints.

In Jack Brabham's team Jack Brabham was the number one driver come what may. On this occasion Jacky Ickx was offered Brabham's car for practice when his own broke down. There was some despondency because practice times were poor and Ickx rather petulantly turned the car down. The reply from Brabham and designer Ron Tauranac was unequivocal. If Ickx did not like it, then he could lump it, which he did. He had won in Germany, won at Oulton Park, he subsequently won the Canadian Grand Prix so it was not beyond the realms of possibility that he could have won at Monza, which would have given him four well deserved wins in a row.

For Jackie Stewart the Italian Grand Prix of 1969 was probably the most significant race of his career. He went into it with the reliability record of his car impaired after the gearbox failure at Nürburgring and battery terminal trouble at Oulton. The impetus of his splendid succession of six Formula 1 wins from seven races in the early part of the season seemed gone. He had not managed to decide the World Championship at Nürburgring. If he failed at Monza he could go on to Canada and then the United States, still perhaps without a clear lead. Then it would be another cliffhanger at Mexico.

It was unlikely. But it was not impossible. Jackie Stewart's arithmetic was as good as anyone else's but he could not forget the disappointments in the past like Indianapolis in 1966 and the catastrophe at Spa a few weeks later.

The Italian Grand Prix meant something of a holiday for me. I took Helen and our children Paul and Mark with their Nanny to the Villa d'Este at Como. This is probably the finest hotel I ever stay at; extravagant perhaps, but something I really enjoy. The service is superb although maybe it was not such a great idea to take the children because the superb service suddenly switched away from mother and father over to them.

The most important factor at Monza seemed to me the choice of gear ratios. Not so much the correct ratio for a fast practice time, but the correct one to win the motor race. It seemed clear that this year especially the usual slipstreaming was going to be very close. There were more Ford engines than ever, which meant more cars with similar performance, and it is a circuit where it is very difficult for one driver to break away from the pack.

Slipstreaming is a technique used in racing where cars have equal or nearly equal performance along the straights. There is an advantage to be gained by following very close behind the car in front. The front car in effect creates a forward rush of air and reduces the wind pressure on the car behind. Consequently, the rear car attains a higher speed than it would in 'clean' air, rather like the cyclist who is 'paced' behind a motorcycle. But just like the cyclist, the rear car can only exploit the advantage by use of a higher gear which allows it to accelerate inside the 'draught' and wind up enough speed to overtake the one in front along the straights. Monza lends itself to the technique which requires very cool nerves with cars literally inches from one another at speeds of around 200 mph. It leads to cars 'bunching' in each other's slipstreams. It also requires drivers to stick closely to the rules of the game because one mistake could involve the others instantly in a multiple collision.

With the Championship at stake as well as the motor race, what we required was a gear ratio for the very last lap. It was obvious that we were all going to be very close. I wanted a gear ratio which would provide an advantage through the final three corners and give extra acceleration across the finishing line.

It takes a very special kind of driving at Monza. Not ability in the ordinary sense.

Smoothness is even more vital. But the problem was not a driving gear ratio, it was choosing the correct one for exiting from the Parabolica. I spent much of practice changing them. Four times in all to get the best performance from the Parabolica up to the finishing line because there, I felt sure, was where the race was going to be won or lost.

Because of this I do not think I achieved the best practice time I could, but the car had been tested on full tanks. I was satisfied and never even tried to pull out a fast one at the end of practice because I felt sure most of the race would be indecisive, and it would all happen on the last lap.

On race day I had driven down with Philip Martin, a London friend of mine who is a sort of professional spectator in his new 6.3 litre Mercedes-Benz. Apart from getting into the circuit one of the biggest problems at Monza is the crowds. People press in on all sides of you; the Italians are most enthusiastic about motor racing. I often had to hide myself in the Dunlop caravan. As usual we had a slight altercation with the officials. On race day I came to the paddock gate and the man in charge would not let me through. 'The "Piloto" badge,' he explained, 'is not amongst the specimens I have here on this board, set up to identify those whom I may let past.' Sure enough, it was not. My protests were in vain. I had my overalls with my name, but it didn't matter, I could not get in. My badge, it seemed, was spurious. Eventually a crowd gathered, containing like any good-natured Italian crowd its share of militant anarchists, who finally persuaded the official that my claim for entry to the paddock was not unreasonable.

At the start of the race I must have touched Denny's front fin in my efforts to get amongst the front row of the grid. I followed Jochen through the Curva Grande, round the two Lesmos and passed him through his slipstream on the straight between the Ascari and the Parabolica. The cars were in a pretty tight bunch. I remained in front, and during the next lap there occurred one of these incidents that illustrate the 'slow motion camera' effect you get in a racing car.

Shortly after I overtook Jochen I caught sight of a tiny movement well down the straight a long way ahead. It was a hare. The cars approached at something like 190 mph into the curve when it suddenly darted out. First it made towards the pack of cars bearing down on it. Then it sprinted right into my path. My right front tyre hit it; there was no question of me deviating even a fraction to avoid it. I would have had an accident and taken half the Italian Grand Prix off the road with me.

My feelings were not entirely humanitarian towards the unfortunate animal, but they were humanitarian towards me. I went through agonies for the next few laps thinking a bone had perhaps lodged in the tyre, or maybe its teeth were being beaten through the tread with every revolution. My acuity of every movement of the car was sharpened and I could hardly take my eyes off the front tyre, or the rear which I watched through the mirror. The shape of the tyre is often the first warning you get of a puncture. The tread goes concave as it deflates, and you have to slow down and stop as smoothly as possible before it overheats or lose control at the next corner.

There was no way out. Jochen was on one side of me, and the edge of the track was on the other, but that hare gave me some anxious moments in the early part of the race.

Jackie Stewart led for 58 of the 68 laps. Or at least he led past the pits. In fact, the lead changed several times on other parts of the circuit, no one will ever know how often. The pack consisted for most of the time of Stewart, Rindt, Hulme, Hill, Beltoise, Courage, McLaren and Siffert.

Rindt usually passed Stewart by coming out of his slipstream before the end of the straight. Stewart would then follow him through the bends on the other side of the circuit, not crowding, but offering the chance of using all the road to see if they could break away from the pack together. Then, just before the final two bends before the start-finish straight, the Parabolica, Stewart would overtake Rindt out of his slipstream and lead past the pits again. The result was that spectators in different places on the circuit had totally different ideas of who was dominating the race. The official record says Stewart, but if you had been doing your lap chart on the Curva Grande you would almost certainly have gained a completely different picture.

The same pattern would be followed with most of the other cars in the pack, either Graham or Piers, or Jochen although it was Jochen most of the time. Interestingly, it seems certain now that Monza is faster without aerofoils. Piers was using them and most of the others were not. Piers, who was driving beautifully was easily the fastest car through the Curva Grande which is one of the most difficult corners in the motor racing world and although he was probably getting superior adhesion there with the aerofoils, that race marked him out as a mature Grand Prix driver. He understands slipstreaming well and his road craft was a good deal better than the Piers Courage we used to know.

The group thinned out a little. Jo Siffert was amongst us for a time, but he fell back and eventually went out with a blown piston.

Monza really shows how drivers behave under pressure. The previous year I was just about to hit the apex at the Ascari at about 180 mph in a similar slipstreaming race when Jo came up the inside in a flash of blue with two wheels on the grass. It really was a scary move, particularly since there was no way he could have passed and all he did was slow us all down momentarily while we got back into shape. Jo tends to live for the moment in these circumstances.

Denny Hulme was amongst us in this year's race although he too fell back with trouble. Denny is very accomplished at sitting back and waiting. He is very patient and waits until it is time to take advantage of the situation and when he does, he does so very decisively. He is ideal at Monza because he is so unflappable.

Jochen and I communicate very well in a close race like this. We even gave each other signals about which side to overtake on. There was no occasion for baulking or stealing each other's line because you just cannot do things like that at Monza speeds.

During the race I tried every way to find out who could beat me and where, finding by experiment that if I went into the Parabolica first I could not be overtaken by any of the group before the start-finish line. I had arranged my gear ratios so that I could take the Parabolica in second gear, which gave me enough flexibility to do almost anything in the corner and still come out in the right rev band to take third gear and then hold fourth past the flag.

Most of the others were in third round there which was good. It meant they did not have quite the same urge because they changed into fifth sooner. This gave them extra speed at the end of the straight and not over the finish line because fifth gear is higher.

The scheme was to slow down the pace of the group through the Parabolica and exploit my second gear to get ahead for the chequered flag. So long as Graham Hill was in the bunch, I was afraid my plan might not work because I would be in a Lotus sandwich. I comforted myself that both Graham and Jochen would be trying to win and not co-operating to thwart me. But Graham dropped out with transmission trouble shortly before the end.

On the last lap, I led past the start-finish line. Jochen passed me going into the Curva Grande and I followed him all the way round into the Parabolica and came out of the slipstream and passed him again. On the last corner of the last lap heroic manouevres are simply not on. So, I braked a little early for the Parabolica. But I had reckoned without Jean-Pierre in the other Matra. He suddenly dived in ahead of Jochen into my slipstream and just as I was committing myself to the corner, there was Jean-Pierre on my inside.

I had to alter my line at the last minute, let him go wide, but put myself out on the loose gravel near the edge of the track. For a moment I thought Jochen was going to get through but he was still behind me. I had to use Jean-Pierre's slipstream, then exploit my fourth gear advantage to overtake him just a fraction before the flag. Jochen followed me and also overtook, but I managed to keep the advantage over him by a few feet, won the race and with it the World Championship.

The tension this race had built up was almost oppressive. For nearly an hour and forty minutes the world's leading half dozen drivers had been battling in one of the most closely fought Grand Prix races ever. But for the bid by Beltoise in the closing moments, it seems likely Stewart would have won by a wider margin than the official eight hundredths of a second. By the time he had completed his cooling down lap and been presented with the Lorenzo Bandini Trophy by the widow of the fine Italian driver killed two years before at Monaco, the crowd had burst on to the track and swarmed round him and Helen in a thoroughly alarming fashion. They sought refuge in an office from which Jackie only escaped through a lavatory into the paddock and the Dunlop transporter, a big 7 ton Austin. This in turn was mobbed by a huge crowd which almost threatened to overturn it. Once again Jackie had to escape, this time with help from some Dunlop men, notably their Garth-like Competitions p.r.o., Ian Norris.

Everybody was delighted with the result and the champagne began to flow at Dunlop's place. I went over to the Ferodo camp where they were holding a party for Harold Theyer, 'their man' who was leaving competitions. Everyone seemed to be celebrating and it went on all evening right through the Dunlop party at the Hotel de la Ville in Monza, yet it still had not registered that I had actually won the World Championship. I knew I had won. I had added up the points. But I did not yet feel a World Champion.

It was not till the following day at the Villa d'Este when I went downstairs to the hall porter and asked him to book a flight to Paris for me on the following Wednesday. He called the airline and said he wanted a first-class reservation for Mr Jackie Stewart ... 'Champion of the World'. I thought, 'That sounds funny.' And for the first time I realised what had happened. This man had thought it worthwhile saying to someone and that brought it home to me.

Soon there were lots of other things. Telephone calls, telegrams, letters, everything. I was very proud when I spoke to my father on the telephone. I could not get through that night but I spoke to him the following day and he sounded like a young man again. He was excited. My mother had been getting flowers addressed to, 'the World Champion's Mum', and all father's own cronies had been telephoning. The Provost of my hometown of Dumbarton had said there was to be a civic reception. My father was perhaps a little melancholy too but rejuvenated by having lived to see me World Champion.

It also brought an enormous amount of work, trying to answer all the letters, which kept my secretary, Ruth Kinnear, very busy at times travelling in aircraft with her notebook to try and stretch the working day by an hour or two.

The ceremonies which followed the World Championship were all extremely pleasing but one or two stand out. First, the British Guild of Motoring Writers elected me Driver of the Year for the second year. Stirling Moss, Jimmy Clark, and Jack Brabham have all gained the honour twice, but this was the first time it had ever been awarded two years running.

Everyone has a feeling of loyalty to their home town and the Dumbarton Civic Reception was a big thrill. I was astonished at the number of people who turned out in the pouring rain to see me with my Formula 2 Matra going through the town behind the pipe band. But the trophy I prized most was given to me at the Scottish Motor Racing Club (of which I am President) Dinner in Edinburgh at the end of November. This is the Jim Clark Memorial Trophy and it was given to me by Jimmy's father. It was very touching. The trophy itself is a beautiful silver helmet and it made me very proud as a Scottish World Champion to get it from the family of Jim Clark. I realised in whose footsteps I was following.

14.

Mosport, The Canadian Grand Prix

Mosport Park, Canada, September 20th, 1969. 2.459 miles to the lap, race distance 90 laps, 221.31 miles. Surprisingly fast undulating circuit with long straights and comparatively slow corners. It lies some 25 miles east of Toronto near Bowmanville on Lake Ontario. There were 20 starters. The lap record was held by Jim Clark in a Lotus-Ford at 1 min. 23.1 sec., a speed of 106.53 mph. The starting grid was as

Rindt (Lotus-Ford) 1.17.9		**Beltoise** (Matra-Ford) 1.17.9		**Ickx** (Brabham-Ford) 1.17.4
	Hulme (McLaren-Ford) 1.18.0		**Stewart** (Matra-Ford) 1.17.9	
Siffert (Lotus-Ford) 1.18.5		**Hill** (Lotus-Ford) 1.18.3		**Brabham** (Brabham-Ford) 1.18.0
	Courage (Brabham-Ford) 1.19.5		**McLaren** (McLaren-Ford) 1.18.5	
Rodriguez (Ferrari) 1.20.5		**Oliver** (BRM) 1.20.2		**Miles** (Lotus-Ford) 1.20.0
	Servoz-Gavin (Matra-Ford) 1.21.4		**Surtees** (BRM) 1.20.6	
Brack (BRM) 1.28.7		**Pease** (Eagle-Climax) 1.28.5		**Lovely** (Lotus-Ford) 1.22.9
	Moser (Brabham-Ford) 1.41.4		**Cordts** (Brabham-Climax) 1.29.7	

follows:

The result was :

1st Jacky Ickx (Brabham-Ford). 1 hour 59 mins. 25.7 sec. 112.76 mph.
2nd Jack Brabham (Brabham-Ford). 2 hours 00 mins. 11.9 sec. 111.91 mph.
3rd Jochen Rindt (Lotus-Ford). 2 hours 00 mins. 17.7 sec. 111.91 mph.
4th Jean-Pierre Beltoise (Matra-Ford) 89 laps
5th Bruce McLaren (McLaren-Ford) 87 laps

6th Johnny Servoz-Gavin (Matra-Ford) 84 laps
7th Pete Lovely (Lotus-Ford) 81 laps
Bill Brack (BRM) 80 laps (still running at finish but unclassified).

Fastest lap: Jacky Ickx (Brabham-Ford) 1 min. 19.1 sec. 114.78 mph.

World Championship points after Mosport: 1st Stewart 60 points.2nd Ickx 31 points.3rd McLaren 26 points. 4th Hill 19 points. 5th Beltoise 18 points. 6th Rindt 13 points. equal Siffert 13 points. 7th Hulme 11 points. 8th Courage 10 points. 9th Brabham 7 points. 10th Amon 4 points. 11th Attwood 3 points. equal Elford 3 points. 12th Surtees 2 points. 13th Brabham 1 point. equal Rodriguez 1 point.

With the World Championship safely won Jackie might have been expected to take the pressure off his racing. Not a bit of it. He fought out every race as hard as ever. He still had a target, which was to win more Grands Prix in a season than anyone else.

I arrived in Canada straight from Albi to do some appearances for Players to help promote the Grand Prix. Promotion for motor racing is still very important in North America because in some places it is still not quite accepted as a mass sport, and Players gave me some very good opportunities to project motor racing as a whole, not just the Grand Prix or Jackie Stewart. This was an occasion where I felt the organisers of the race were prepared to use drivers to publicise it to very good effect. In fact, I felt overworked. By race day I was quite tired; better than being under-employed.

Some idea of the professional scale of race promotion in Toronto can be gained from Jackie Stewart's programme. On arrival he did a golf tournament reception, then a press conference, then some TV and radio interviews. He went to a TV studio to take part in a live sports programme and arrived back at his hotel after midnight on the day he had flown the Atlantic. Next day began at 7.30 am for a breakfast time TV show, then two radio shows, a public appearance and a drive through Toronto in the Mosport Circuit's pace car. At the Civic Centre around lunch time, he met the Mayor, was presented with a book about the city, and inaugurated Toronto Grand Prix week. He visited a city store and did yet another half hour TV interview.

This was followed by a meeting with a journalist from one of the leading Toronto newspapers and then another appearance at what was known as the Jackie Stewart Night. Highland Dancers and Bagpipes were included mainly for the benefit of Toronto's large Scottish population. A late conference with the promotors ended a second day's work.

A third day was filled with a Go-Kart race called the 'Wee-Prix' with disc jockeys from the Toronto area at lunch time, which Jackie only won by what he describes '... a little help.' In the evening there was another TV show called 'The Hot Seat' where he endured half an hour's grilling by three leading journalists. It was a full programme which did much to ensure the success of the race and draw good crowds to Mosport.

The GPDA had asked for quite a few improvements to be made at Mosport. Some parts of the circuit were not too good. Kerbs were needed all round which could not be done in time although they did seal off the edge of some corners which helped considerably. They had been working on the track right up to the week of practice and the road was very dirty to begin with.

Choosing gear ratios was always difficult. We tried to get them right the first day of untimed practice and on the morning of the official day got down to a fairly competitive time. But just as we were going out to try for the front row of the grid, the engine broke. Jacky Ickx was quickest, and then came Jean-Pierre, Jochen, and me all with identical times, 1.17.9. I had done my time last, which put me on the second row with Denny Hulme. Jacky had done the time I felt I should have achieved on that circuit, but my car was wheeled away before I could satisfy myself, I could match it. I was only able to console myself with a few laps in the four-wheel drive car.

After the first day's practice we had the Grand Prix Ball where Players paid Rob Walker a great and very well-deserved compliment with a presentation which several drivers endorsed with a short speech. Graham Hill as ever stole the show because of course he was still World Champion.

I spent the evening before the race talking to Rolex dealers and went back to the track early on race morning and put in a few laps to ensure the new engine which had been installed overnight had no oil leaks or other disasters.

There are always lots of Scottish exiles at Canadian races. You can see their flags round the circuit, and they are always encouraging me to uphold the honour of the old country, so I was anxious to try and do well. Yet I have never done well in Canada and this race was unfortunately no exception.

From the second row of the grid Jackie was fourth at the end of lap 1, third on laps 2, 3, and 4, second on lap 5, and took the lead on lap 6 from Rindt. Ickx pulled up behind him on lap 8. Two laps later Stewart caught up and collided with Al Pease, the Canadian driver in an Eagle. It was Pease's second collision of the day - he was to have several more. It was Jackie's first, but he too was to be involved in another, probably the most controversial accident of the season.

Jacky Ickx was snapping at my heels, although once again I seemed to have a fairly good set of gear ratios except on one corner where he was able to make up quite a lot of ground. He lost considerably on the hairpin but his new Goodyears were superior on medium speed comers and although he seemed able to make up any leeway, I could out-drag him on the straight and felt fairly confident I could keep him at bay for the remainder of the race.

Unfortunately, at around one third distance I came up behind Bill Brack's BRM on Turn 1, lapping him and slowing a fraction which allowed the Brabham to catch up. Along the straight before Turn 2, I overtook the BRM and headed for the corner. Turn 2 is an off-camber, downhill, left hander with a concealed apex. That is, the apex where you clip the edge of the road is out of sight over the hill. It is a comer where you just do not overtake even if a car is 5 seconds a lap slower than you. It is a fast comer that drops away sharply and there is only one line you can take. Any deviation will land you in the dirt at the edge if nothing worse.

How Jacky misjudged it I do not know, but he hit me and immediately the car spun out of control and went down through a vacant space which the GPDA had asked to be cleared of a dangerous-looking bank. I ended up at the bottom of the hill in a great cloud of choking dust. The throttle cable had broken because the dust had jammed in the slides during the accident and when I opened the throttle to restart the engine it pulled the nipple out of the cable behind the pedal.

I got out of the car and saw there was no damage apart from some fragments broken off the rim of a rear wheel - it would have been able to continue. I undid the accelerator cable and brought it into the cockpit so that I could have worked it as a hand throttle to get back to the pits. But the battery was slightly flat and would not turn the engine. This is a fault of the Cosworth. The starter motor becomes hot in the course of a race and after several tries, I had to give up and get the car off the road and out of the way in case someone else followed me.

There was nothing for it but a very disappointed walk back to the pits. I was annoyed because I had been leading my seventh Grand Prix. I knew Jacky had not done it intentionally but I did feel he had been rather over-enthusiastic in his efforts to get past.

The MS 80 with the wings abbreviated.

Stewart and Ken Tyrrell confer during a test session at Brands Hatch.

He had tried a similar manoeuvre a few laps earlier when we were lapping Pete Lovely. I had let Lovely into a corner ahead of us and he then waved both of us through, but Jacky had tried to go round on the inside while I was passing on the outside and there simply was not enough room for three cars abreast. He seemed to be in a rather over confident frame of mind that day.

I told Ken all about the accident and then went on ABC Television and talked to Phil Hill and Chris Economaki. Jacky apologised afterwards both on the public address and personally in Bruce McLaren's caravan while I was chatting to David Phipps, so honour was satisfied. He restarted after the accident and won the race clearly, with Jack Brabham second after wearing down Jochen, who came in third. It was a very successful day for the Brabham team and probably restored some of their faith in Ickx despite the Monza incident as well as his precipitate announcement that he would be driving for Ferrari in 1970.

15.

Watkins Glen, the United States Grand Prix

Watkins Glen, USA, October 8th, 1969. 2.3 miles to the lap, race distance 108 laps, 248.4 miles. Situated in the hills overlooking Seneca Lake above the town of Watkins Glen, Shuyler County, in upstate New York, this short road circuit is a succession of fast sweeping bends.

There were 18 starters, including Bruce McLaren whose car broke down on the warming-up lap. The Formula 1 lap record was held by Jackie Stewart in a Matra-Ford at 1 min. 5.22 sec., a speed of 126.96 mph, and the Can-Am lap record was held by Denny Hulme in a McLaren Chevrolet M8B at 1 min. 2.6 sec., a speed of 132.27 mph. The starting grid was as follows:

	Hulme (McLaren-Ford) 1.3.65		**Rindt** (Lotus-Ford) 1.3.62
Hill (Lotus-Ford) 1.4.05		**Stewart** (Matra-Ford) 1.3.77	
	McLaren (McLaren-Ford) 1.4.22		**Siffert** (Lotus-Ford) 1.4.06
Ickx (Brabham-Ford) 1.4.32		**Beltoise** (Matra-Ford) 1.4.29	
	Brabham (Brabham-Ford) 1.4.86		**Courage** (Brabham-Ford) 1.4.58
Rodriguez (Ferrari) 1.5.94		**Surtees** (BRM) 1.5.06	
	Oliver (BRM) 1.6.55		**Andretti** (Lotus-Ford) 1.6.52
Lovely (Lotus-Ford) 1.7.55		**Servoz-Gavin** (Matra-Ford) 1.7.13	
	Eaton (BRM) 1.11.27		**Moser** (Brabham-Ford) 1.8.20

The result was:

1st Jochen Rindt (Lotus-Ford). 1 hour 57 mins. 56.84 sec. 126.36 mph.

2nd Piers Courage (Brabham-Ford). 1 hour 58 mins. 43.83 sec.

3rd John Surtees (BRM) 106 laps.

4th Jack Brabham (Brabham-Ford) 106 laps.

5th Pedro Rodriguez (Ferrari) 101 laps.

6th Silvio Moser (Brabham-Ford) 98 laps.

7th Johnny Servoz-Gavin (Matra-Ford) 92 laps.

Fastest lap, Jochen Rindt (Lotus-Ford) 1 min. 4.34 sec.128.69 mph.

World Championship points after Watkins Glen: 1st Stewart 60 points. 2nd lckx 31 points. 3rd McLaren 26 points. 4th Rindt 22 points. 5th Hill 19 points. 6th Beltoise 18 points. 7th Courage 16 points. 8th Siffert 13 points. 9th Hulme 11 points. 10th Brabham 10 points. 11th Surtees 6 points. 12th Amon 4 points. 13th Attwood 3 points. equal Elford 3 points. equal Rodriguez 3 points. 16th Servoz-Gavin 1 point. 17th Moser 1 point.

If there is one race in the season more worth winning than any other, it is the United States Grand Prix at Watkins Glen. Even in this most beautiful part of America, ablaze with autumn colours, prize money at 'The Glen' is still everything.

Most races offer two sources of income for entrants. There is prize money and there is starting money. The prize money is just what it says and the sums are usually quite small, a few hundred pounds perhaps. Starting money is also what it says, money for starting. Its proportions vary according to how much an organiser thinks you are worth, their assessment of the crowd-drawing capacity of car and driver. The agreed scale depends largely on the previous year's World Championship standing.

Thus, a top team can expect between £1,500 and £2,000 per car, of which £500 to £750 goes to the driver to cover his expenses. The driver's actual earnings are likely to come mostly from retainers, and bonuses from tyre, oil, and accessory companies probably plus a proportion of his car's earnings.

The United States Grand Prix is run on different lines. Instead of prize money and starting money the cash is prize money only. The game is to win, not just start. In 1969 the prize fund was $209,000, and finishers were paid down to 20th place as follows:

1st $50,000.	*6th $9,000.*	*11th $6,900*	*16th $6,400.*
2nd $20,000.	*7th $8,500.*	*12th $6,800.*	*17th $6,300.*
3rd $12.000.	*8th $8,000.*	*13th $6,700.*	*18th $6,200.*
4th $10,000	*9th $7,500.*	*14th $6,600.*	*19th $6,100.*
5th $9,500.	*10th $7,000.*	*15th $6,500.*	*20th $6,000.*

Fastest race lap earned the Onyx Trophy and $2,000. Fastest practice lap, $1,000. That Fifty Thousand Dollars for first place was far higher than even top starting money plus a win anywhere else. This race is the richest of the Formula 1 season. In view of the unusual financial arrangements, unique in Grand Prix racing but common practice in the United States, Jackie and Ken agreed on this occasion to pool their costs and split the profit.

I have no strong preference for either a starting money scheme or a prize money system. Whatever happens, the first-place man will always make money, so that drivers with a chance of doing well generally favour the prize money system but run the risk of winding up with no one to race against. Prize money only races can hurt small teams, or a driver who has an unsuccessful year or two with some bad cars. That can happen.

Another thing that concerns me is that we drivers have been asking race organisers to use us more for promoting the races. We felt we had an obligation to do more for our starting money than merely start. But under the prize system, if organisers want to use us for anything other than just racing, they are going to have to pay for our time.

Both ways can have advantages for the very small teams, like say Silvio Moser, who owns his own Brabham-Ford and must work on a small budget. Teams like this can be better with a guaranteed income, the trouble is that this is small in comparison with the outlay to set up in racing. Small teams and less well-known drivers do not get much starting money, yet they are sure of something.

Prize-money-only on the other hand, can help a small team to do well simply through finishing races. With discretion and steady driving, you can often make sure of finishing. If you were 7th every time you could end a season (on US Grand Prix figures) with over $100,000, but not a single Championship point. Even half this would still be wealth beyond the dreams of avarice for teams who are now rubbing along with 'guaranteed' starting money.

If every prize fund matched the US Grand Prix's, the small teams would be all right.

Watkins Glen ought to encourage its young, festive atmosphere. Every year crowds of youngsters camp within the circuit for the whole weekend and laugh and drink and have parties. A music festival or something could be run in conjunction with motor racing. They get 100,000 - odd people there and if it is possible to get that number of customers just for a race, how many more would

Bruce McLaren, Denny Hulme, Graham Hill, Silvio Moser, Jo Stiffert, Jackie Stewart, Piers Courage, Jochen Rindt, Vic Elford, Jean-Pierre Beltoise, Jacky Ickx and Chris Amon.

Jackie with his chief mechanic, Max Rutherford.

they get if they threw in a music festival as well. The organisers have established a great tradition there and all they need to do now is improve the facilities a bit. They need to make it easier to watch the race, and also improve the safety of spectators.

Graham Hill's accident was made worse by the earth banks which the GPDA had asked to be moved. Earth banks become ramps that launch a car into the air. The Watkins Glen Grand Prix Corporation had worked hard to get their prize money up to over $200,000 and of course the drivers appreciated that - it was going to be our money. But we would rather they took twenty or thirty thousand dollars of it and made the track safer for the spectators and us alike. Ickx went off the road in practice and he could easily have gone into the crowd.

Graham has been criticised for not having his seat belts on when he crashed. He had climbed out of the car to push it to a hill and restart after a spin. But the driver cannot do up the belts we use in single seaters without help from outside. I can't do mine up. So, Graham was not merely being careless. Jochen took a look at the car afterwards and said that the monocoque had stood up to the impact well, 'It was in good shape to be inside in an accident.' But of course, Graham was not inside and had severe leg injuries which was very upsetting for everyone. I am afraid it took the shine off Jochen's first Grand Prix victory.

My engine went off form on the warming-up lap. I came in before going on to the grid to see if there was anything that could be done. I thought it might be a plug lead adrift or something trivial. We changed the metering unit mixture on the fuel injection, but it was neither that nor the plugs. The miss got worse and the car was not on full power from the start.

Rindt led the US Grand Prix until the 11th lap with Jackie in close pursuit, overtaking him, only to be repassed going into Turn One 9 laps later. At first Jackie kept up, but within a few more laps the gap opened from a few feet to yards, and finally the Matra went out on lap 35 with a massive oil leak from the rear main engine bearing.

If anyone had deserved to win a Grand Prix it was Jochen, yet this was his first. He was undoubtedly the most competitive driver of the season, a very talented driver with whom I enjoy racing very much. We are almost next-door neighbours; we live about 300 yards apart, Helen and Nina are friendly and our children play together.

Jochen and I not only race against each other in Formula1 but in Formula 2 as well. We often say that one of these days we are going to come together and have each other off the road. We are driving the backside off each other, on the limit all the time and sooner or later we must get our wheels tangled.

Jochen is a very hard competitor. When he thinks he has an advantage he really works hard on it. But if he thinks he is losing on something, I always feel he tends to slacken off a bit. He seems to reach a point where, if he feels he is not going to make it, instead of keeping up he drops back. This is unlike most drivers, yet there are very few with the natural talent or natural ability Jochen has. He is probably the most talented driver I race against. He is a mature driver. He is a steady driver, a fast driver, and a very calculating driver. Most of all he keeps cool when he is in a tight spot in a racing car. His ability is of a very natural sort.

I like Jochen a lot as a person. He is hard; he had a very difficult youth, having lost both parents in the war when he was only a year old, but I admire his abilities. He was brought up in Graz, Austria where he is something of a National Hero. He has done a great deal for motor racing and is a great sporting personality, recognised as such wherever he goes.

I genuinely hope Jochen does get success. Not too much of it, but I hope he gets it.

Having won the American Grand Prix, the flood gates of Formula 1 wins are open for him.

16.

Mexico City, the Mexican Grand Prix

Mexico City, Mexico, October 19th, 1969.

3.107 miles to the lap, race distance 65 laps, 201.94 miles. The circuit is a long artificial track with a large number of slow and medium speed corners. There were 17 starters, the lap record was held by Jo Siffert in a Lotus-Ford at 1.44.23, a speed of 107.26 mph. The starting grid was as follows:

	Hulme (McLaren-Ford) 1.3.65		**Rindt** (Lotus-Ford) 1.3.62
Hill (Lotus-Ford) 1.4.05		**Stewart** (Matra-Ford) 1.3.77	
	McLaren (McLaren-Ford) 1.4.22		**Siffert** (Lotus-Ford) 1.4.06
Ickx (Brabham-Ford) 1.4.32		**Beltoise** (Matra-Ford) 1.4.29	
	Brabham (Brabham-Ford) 1.4.86		**Courage** (Brabham-Ford) 1.4.58
Rodriguez (Ferrari) 1.5.94		**Surtees** (BRM) 1.5.06	
	Oliver (BRM) 1.6.55		**Andretti** (Lotus-Ford) 1.6.52
Lovely (Lotus-Ford) 1.7.55		**Servoz-Gavin** (Matra-Ford) 1.7.13	
	Eaton (BRM) 1.11.27		**Moser** (Brabham-Ford) 1.8.20

The result was :

1st Denny Hulme (McLaren-Ford) 1 hour 54 mins. 08.80 sec. 106.15 mph.

2nd Jacky Ickx (Brabham-Ford). 1 hour 54 mins. 11.36 sec.

3rd Jack Brabham (Brabham-Ford). 1 hour 54 mins. 47.28 sec.

4th Jackie Stewart (Matra-Ford). 1 hour 54 mins. 55.84 sec.

5th Jean-Pierre Beltoise (Matra-Ford). 1 hour 55 mins. 47.32 sec.

6th Jackie Oliver (BRM) 63 laps.

7th Pedro Rodriguez (Ferrari) 63 laps.

8th Johnny Servoz-Gavin (Matra-Ford) 62 laps

9th Pete Lovely (Lotus-Ford) 62 laps

10th Piers Courage (Brabham-Ford) 61 laps.

11th Silvio Moser (Brabham-Ford) 60 laps (not running at finish)

Fastest Lap; Jacky Ickx (Brabham-Ford) 1 min. 43.05 sec. 108.53 mph.

World Championship points after Mexico City: 1st Stewart 63 points. 2nd Ickx 37 points. 3rd McLaren 26 points. 4th Rindt 22 points. 5th Hulme 20 points. equal Beltoise 20 points 7th Hill 19 points. 8th Courage 16 points. 9th Siffert 15 points. 10th Brabham 14 points. 11th Surtees 6 points. 12th Amon 4 points. 13th Attwood 3 points. equal Elford 3 points. equal Rodriguez 3 points. 16th Servoz-Gavin 1 point. equal Moser 1 point. equal Oliver 1 point.

Unfortunately, a tyre company who will be nameless brought out a new compound for this race, which was faster than anything we had, or Firestone had. That narrows the field. All the cars on this compound went quickly. I went as fast as I could; I got a very good start and led for five laps, being pressed yet knowing I was not going to be able to remain ahead of Jacky Ickx, Denny Hulme, and Jack Brabham.

It was unfortunate that Jacky chose to pass me under the yellow flag. We came across the accident which took place between Piers Courage and Jo Siffert at the hairpin, the yellow flag was being waved as we entered, I raised my hand and slowed down. Jacky shot through on the inside, which was a bit naughty. People could have been in the middle of the road or clearing away wreckage or, for all we knew, lying somewhere injured. With Mexican crowd control, almost anything could have been happening there and we were not in a position to see what had occurred.

I am sure Jacky was going to pass me anyway. My car lacked downright adhesion. It was not a tyre construction problem, the Goodyear compound just had more 'stick', particularly through the Esses where there were quick changes of direction; the rubber seemed to 'recover' quickly from opposing cornering forces. Jacky, Denny, Jack, and even Silvio Moser with his old Brabham were taking distance off me. I came up behind Silvio, who races with a series 8 Ford Cosworth engine in a car which is slightly out of date, and I thought he was going to hold me up. I caught him just after the hairpin where you get five corners immediately following one another. 'There's a second and a half gone through following Silvio,' I thought. In fact, I came out of the series a second and a half farther back than I had been. That really brought home to me that things were not quite as they should be.

I drove a hard race from start to finish, as fast as I could, but there was just nothing I could do. I could not catch Jack Brabham even though his engine was off song. It was not responding properly coming out of corners and I still could not keep up the ability of the Goodyears to hold themselves through the fast swerves was so marked. The result was a fine win for Denny, his first of the season, at least in Grands Prix.

Denny must have lost count of all the other races he won in 1969, particularly in Can-Am. By midsummer we were all going to him when we wanted a loan and by the end of the year we heard he practically owned the whole of the United States. Yet he continues to meander along with his hands dangling down beside him. He is a big, strong man Denny, a quiet man whom somehow the press has never been able to make out. He was a very modest World Champion, even though he won it and the Can-Am the same year, which is a tremendous feat. He is generally modest, does not want to appear obtrusive, yet on the track he is a very fast, well-regulated driver and off it a very nice person.

His father won a VC in Crete during the war and comes over to Europe maybe once every two or three years and he too looks a very strong character. One day, Denny says he is going to blow the lot and go right away over to New Zealand and get on to some island and never leave it. And I can see him doing it. That's the way it is with Denny.

In Mexico, the altitude is an old problem. I did not do a great deal of running around there because I have found it does show up with me. I enjoy Mexico except having to discipline myself with the food. I went there some years ago and contracted the dreaded 'Montezuma's Revenge' tummy which most of the Grand Prix circus have had. I now eat steaks without potatoes or salad, and drink Coca-Cola exclusively. It is an imposition, but you cannot risk your performance in a race for an ice-cream or fruit salad.

We stay at the Camino Reale, which must be one of the most modern hotels in the world and architecturally very striking. It takes up two Mexico City blocks, is only three or four storeys high but sprawls so much they give you a little map to find your way round the corridors, bars and seven restaurants as well as five swimming pools. It is also very quiet. The most noise is from the water bubbling and splashing through the fountains. The people are enjoyable, more so now that I have come to know so many of them.

One of the highlights of the event is the wonderful party which is run at Raymond O'Farrell's home a couple of nights before the race. It is a beautiful house, full of antique furniture. O'Farrell himself is a great tycoon in Mexico and lives very luxuriously. This is the end of the motor racing season, and everything has a special end-of-term atmosphere. The party is a big affair with colourful Mexicans, and members of diplomatic staffs in Mexico. Everything is on the grand scale.

The track at Mexico is one I like, although it always seems strewn with stray spectators and dogs and kids and I just hope nobody ever has a big shunt there that involves any of them. We complain to the authorities about it every year and while things have improved - they no longer sit at the edge of the track with their feet on the roadway there is a long way to go before they have a safe circuit. I do love Mexico City and its environs although there no longer seems enough time to go sightseeing at places like this. The pace of everything has increased so much since I went there first in 1965. Helen came with me in 1969 for the first time and she enjoyed the social side very much. There was a magnificent banquet the night after the race on which the club must have spent a fortune. There is an emotional quality about speeches people make on this occasion because you are all together for the last time in the year, everyone with whom you have shared a year's racing. You have shared dramatic and amusing experiences with them, now you are all going to separate and go back to different countries, do different things until Kyalami the following year.

By then, it will be different. Drivers will have changed teams, there may be new faces. And there will never be another 1969 season.

17.

Conclusion

When it was all over there was not much time to collect one's thoughts. There seemed so much to be done. Appearances, invitations, and congratulations continued, all very welcome but physically as exhausting as the motor racing season.

During November, 1969, Jackie's diary read as follows: 1st and 2nd, shooting in Spain with the Crown Prince. 3rd and 4th, press interviews in Geneva. 5th, London for a celebration lunch. 6th and 7th, Glasgow Motor Show at Kelvin Hall with a number of receptions, appearances, and dinners including one, always notable, with the Association of Scottish Motoring Writers aboard the Carrick, the 1864 Clipper City of Adelaide moored at the Broomielaw as an RNVR Club. On the 8th was a Mechanics' Dinner in London. 9th, recording session in London, fly to Geneva. 10th, 11th, and 12th in Paris. 13th 'Man of the Year' dinner in London. 15th, 16th, filming with Elf, the petrol company in Paris. 17th Geneva. 18th, Champion Spark Plug lunch in London, and a recording session. 19th, 20th, appearance at the Jochen Rindt Racing Car Show in Vienna. 21st, Scottish Motor Racing Club dinner in Edinburgh. 22nd, Dumbarton Civic Reception. 23rd golf at Turnberry, 24th and 25th, Geneva. 26th, appearance at Munich Jochen Rindt Show. 27th Ferodo dinner, London. 28th, Guild of Motoring Writers dinner and presentation of Driver of the Year award, London. 29th, recording session, 30th, return to Geneva.

The time in London was almost wholly exhausted by press interviews, business meetings. filming, and brief visits to follow the progress of his 1970 racing car. Most of the trips he makes by commercial airline, flying Pan-American when he can, but also using Swissair and BEA frequently for his European trips. Early in December he flew BOAC on two return trips to Johannesburg within the space of ten days. Sometimes he uses small executive aircraft, occasionally chartering his friend Sir John Whitmore's Jet Commander.

The pace was a little exhausting, but I am sure that putting the World Champion on show is good for motor racing, it is good for sponsors and they are the people who make it all commercially feasible. They, together with Ken Tyrrell, put together my 1969 team.

Matra International is really no more than a registered trade name for entering the cars. The team remains the Tyrrell Racing Organisation, which is wholly owned by Ken Tyrrell. The mechanics were Max Rutherford, a New Zealander whose job was to organise their work; Roger Hill another New Zealander in charge of car preparation with joint overall responsibility for the team; Keith Boshier from Guildford, Alan Stait, a north countryman; Ken (Eric) Sykes also from Guildford, and Marcel Vieuble, a Matra mechanic with special responsibility for Jean-Pierre's car. Bruno Morin, a Matra chassis engineer who travelled with us was a nuclear physicist as well as an engineer. He was responsible for liaison between the team and the factory, a vital factor in our success. We used his engineering a good deal but had less need for his nuclear physics.

The Matra airbourne at the Nürburgring.

Jackie's favourite headgear.

Jackie and Helen at Monaco.

Jackie is as successful a fisherman as he is a racing driver.

All the mechanics attend all the races and once the season starts, the only way they have any time off is if some fly home and have a day or two clear before the team's Leyland transporter (which started life as one of the famous Cuba buses and was rescued from the bottom of the Thames) arrives back at headquarters in Ripley, Surrey.

Throughout the year we had eight Cosworth DFV engines, two older ones known as 8 series, and six of the newer 9 series with revised camshafts and new timing gears, which could be revved an extra 500 rpm to a maximum of 10,000. The price of each Ford Cosworth V8, designed by the brilliant Keith Duckworth is £7,500, so you can imagine the investment involved in preparing a racing team for a season. Race preparation means expensive engine overhauls at frequent intervals. In fact, the engine is virtually renewed for every race. The previous race's engine may be used during practice and the team's whole complement of engines is taken to each race and changed over if they misbehave during practice.

The addition to the team was MS 84 which was built to explore the possibilities of four-wheel drive. Development was difficult because by the time the car was completed the season was well under way and with Formula 2 events and only two weeks between Grands Prix, there was just no time to do any useful work on it.

Test and development work was done on the two-wheel drive cars during the year, at Kyalami, Zandvoort, Silverstone and Oulton Park. In 1968 we also used the Bugatti circuit at Le Mans because it was so convenient to the Matra works. We try to have test sessions at circuits where a Grand Prix is going to be held a short time before and this can be valuable in 'playing oneself in'. But the long sessions at Kyalami for example do not significantly add to a driver's knowledge of a circuit. You will never know much more about a track after 500 laps that you will not know after 50. The exceptions to this rule of course are Nürburgring and to a lesser extent Clermont.

All the major work on the car was done at Matra's works at Velizy near Paris. When, for example, the car was shunted at Silverstone it went back to the works to be rebuilt, otherwise all the race preparation was done at Ripley by Ken's mechanics. During races, Ken managed the pit and timed me, while Bruno timed Jean-Pierre. Norah kept the lap chart which is the difficult bit. Ken's son, Kenneth, who flies as a second officer for BEA in Tridents, usually managed to get his duties to coincide with races in Europe, and he invariably brings as good a weather forecast with him as anyone can get.

Teams have to take safety seriously. Quite apart from it being better to have your driver alive and well, there is the cost of an accident. Take the Mosport crash. The GPDA had asked for the earth bank to be removed from Turn 2 in case a car went off the road. The bank was removed and when I was hit from behind, the car went out of control and right across the vacant piece of ground that had been cleared. Ken knows I will not put cars off the road often during a season, but this is motor racing and here I went off through someone else's mistake. If the bank had still been there the car would have been launched into space and there is no way I could have come out of it safely. Even if I had, the car would certainly have been wrecked. Ken might have had a £30,000 write-off on his hands. Two or three of these in a season would put anybody out of business and that would not be a good thing for me or motor racing or anyone. Everyone makes mistakes but safety precautions must be taken to save cars from writing themselves off unnecessarily.

Once again Matra International provided me with a Formula 2 drive and again John Coombs managed it. We did not do many races but began at Thruxton where I was second to Jochen on the first outing of his new Lotus, completely fresh, light and good looking. Ours on the other hand was a three-year-old design, the car itself was two years old, heavy, and we had no opportunity for fitting wider wheels, or embarking on test and development. We had our hands full with Formula 1. The policy, remember, was to try and win the World Championship and almost everything else took second place. There had been a big investment of time and money, I had foresworn Indianapolis and even some business activities to get the Grand Prix car competitive as possible. Frankly, the Formula 2 programme suffered as a result. Development of a Formula 2 car can be just as demanding as for Formula 1 and there were not enough days in the week for a team of our size to do both.

Jochen also had a very superior Firestone tyre and even half a second a lap is very difficult to get back off someone like him. In Formula 1 there was additional opposition to consider besides Jochen, but in Formula 2 he was the chief opponent and dominated most of the races.

I had to drive very hard. It was nine-tenths or even tentenths all the way to try and keep up. Now this is a very satisfying way of racing because you know you are getting the very maximum out of the car and stretching yourself to the limit. Thruxton was a good example. I felt I had driven better at Thruxton than almost anywhere else in the season, except possibly another F2 race, the Nürburgring. I started Thruxton on the front row of the grid alongside Bill

Ivy who was on Firestones in his ex-Winkelmann Brabham. He was driving extremely well but relatively inexperienced in car racing. He was already a motorcycle champion having won the 125cc title in 1967 and in 1968 was first to lap the TT course at 100 mph in one of these tiny machines. I pulled out a reasonable lead at first, but Jochen who was also on Firestones kept chopping my lead down until he finally passed and drew away. There was no way I could stay with him round corners. I could do most things to keep up with him, he did not out-brake me or out-accelerate me, there was no measurable difference in our cars' performance, except in roadholding.

Thruxton was new to me and I found it difficult to learn, because of the false apexes, double apexes and blind corners where you had to aim the car at a point you could not immediately see. It would be difficult for a driver new to Formula 2 to find his way round Thruxton. The evenly matched cars mean it is hard to find ways of taking half a second off here, or half a second off there simply by driving faster. It has lots of fast and medium speed corners; they are the difficult ones. There are very few slow corners. You have a great deal of satisfaction through being able to balance the car right on the absolute limit and knowing that you personally were wholly satisfied with the job you were doing. This does not often happen in motor racing but Thruxton was an occasion where it did. I felt I had gone as fast as I could on that circuit on that day, with that car and those tyres. I came second to Jochen, but feel sure I gained as much personal satisfaction from it as he did.

Formula 2 clears a lot of air. You get some drivers who enter it and feel they have 'arrived', and while I do not want to sound disparaging it is difficult to master. Both 1968 and 1969 were dominated by Jochen who was being pushed all the way for his wins. Formula 2 has been getting less worthwhile for many professional drivers and while I expect Jochen will remain in it, you may find that he does not have the same pressure from behind. He may not be going quite so fast and some of the better amateur drivers will be able to close up on him. Formula 2's stock might go up as a result and so might the stock of some drivers, but they could easily be misleading themselves.

My best win in Formula 2 was at the Nürburgring. I was able to pull away and win, which is always good, but especially good at the 'Ring ... the car was most beautifully set up, the gear ratios were right beyond belief, everything was right, and I was very happy to win and take the lap record. It gave me confidence that with everything going in my favour, on a good, demanding circuit, I was still competitive with anyone.

One of the highlights of the Formula 2 season, and in fact one of the great losses of the year, was Bill Ivy. First and foremost, Bill was a fantastic character. A flamboyant youngster with a tremendous sense of humour he created a stir from the very beginning. He came into motor racing with his very long hair, far longer than mine, and his Maserati Ghibli. He would arrive with a retinue of gorgeous girls and quite a lot of people took him quite the wrong way. 'Oh dear', they thought, 'Whatever is motor racing coming to. First Jackie Stewart and now this.'

Bill never changed. Other people fitted in with him. You could hardly imagine anything further from Eton and the aristocracy, yet Bill was acceptable to every level of society that you find in modem motor racing. His enormous charm made up for things which in some people's eyes might have been considered to be breaches of etiquette.

After the Nürburgring race in which he had put up an astonishing practice time and then crashed, he appalled the top table personnel at the end-of-race ball. It was composed of impeccably dressed and very dignified, upper-crust Germans with their wives. Bill began making off with their bottles of wine. It might have been a difficult situation, but Bill's charm once again won them over. And they were not people who would normally be well-disposed to a very cheeky, little, long-haired English racing driver. Bill was going to be a top-class driver. It was the first time he had driven a car on the Nürburgring and his performance was a great feat, far more difficult than being quick in a sports car or anything of a more amenable nature. Bill gave us a hilarious evening's entertainment. He wound up dancing with an enormous blonde girl and took advantage of his five feet height to plant his head firmly between her breasts.

Everyone loved Bill in his short career amongst us, and it was very sad that he was killed practising a 4-cylinder Czechoslovak Jawa cycle race in East Germany.

The Formula 1 races which did not count for the World Championship were significant in different ways. The Race of Champions at Brands Hatch came a fortnight after South Africa and we brought out MS 80 on its first race outing and won. I did not think the car handled well at first, it had a lot of bad habits which took a long time to eradicate. They showed up at Brands Hatch in a very nasty way. It 'darted'. You got it to the breakaway point, just where it began to slide through a corner and all of a sudden it decided to make its own way. It became thoroughly bad-mannered, yet it drew ahead for most of the race even though I never had a real hot lap. It still gave the season a great start.

Silverstone on the other hand was a bit of a fiasco. It rained and the same bad habits we experienced at Brands Hatch were exaggerated in the rain to the point where I decided the car was dangerous. Apart from not having wheel rims of the correct size for wet weather tyres I would not have wanted to drive it in the rain.

I had to take the gamble of starting from the back row of the grid with MS 10, which was slightly absurd. There I was, having had the fastest lap in practice and yet choosing to go to the back of the grid and trying to get through the field in pouring rain. 'But', I thought, 'here I am with my Dunlop wet weather tyres and the old MS 10, I'm going to blow them all off.'

Eventually, after what I felt was some keen driving Ken gave me a signal, a Minus on Brabham, indicating the number of seconds I was behind Brabham. 'Ah, I thought, I'm second. It's a long race, I'll try and wear away the gap.' But Brabham kept drawing ahead. I felt I was not going to catch up and if I tried any harder I was going to do something silly. I eased off to establish what I fondly imagined to be second place and Jochen passed me, which I thought made me third. Then about 15 laps from the end I found out I was 5th. Ken had only been giving me Minuses and not my place, perhaps he did not think I deserved it that day. I put on a spurt to catch Piers, then I caught Jacky finally reaching third miles behind the leaders.

The Gold Cup at Oulton Park was also disappointing. I set fastest lap in practice and felt I had the race under control when the battery terminal broke off. I went out again after the pit stop to have a good old thrash to catch Jacky and then another to catch Jochen even though I was several laps behind.

This was one of the occasions where I had to acknowledge the force of Ken's argument about non-championship races. The mechanics had been working very hard, the Gold Cup came between the German Grand Prix and Monza, and Ken was anxious they should have a rest. I wanted to use the four-wheel drive car because I felt it would be significant to try it in the wet. But the engine blew in practice. Ken would not have it changed. It was not a championship race and he wanted to use the time as a breathing space. Tony Rolt encouraged me. Our four-wheel drive system was based on his Ferguson Formula, but Ken was adamant and the two-wheel drive car had to be used instead. He had promised the mechanics an easy time at Oulton, and he would not break his word to them under any circumstances. You had to admit to the wisdom of his industrial relations.

It was a great season. It was a great thrill to win the World Championship. It may be called the Driver's Championship but it depends on many, many people both in the team and out of it. They make up a pyramid that starts with the little group who are with the car on the track. Next down the pyramid you get the trade representatives from Dunlop, Ferodo, Girling, Armstrong, Lucas, and Autolite. Then come the manufacturers and the suppliers, and the people who supply services. There are travel agents and shippers and race organisers and marshals and firemen and ambulancemen, and others who take the money at the turnstiles, the whole army on whom motor racing depends for running itself.

Most of all there are the spectators. And the sponsors. It is a big pyramid.

Illustrations:

Printed in Great Britain
by Amazon

57658557R10096